Machine Learning for Beginners 2019

The Ultimate Guide to Artificial Intelligence, Neural Networks, and Predictive Modelling (Data Mining Algorithms & Applications for Finance, Business & Marketing)

by Matt Henderson

© Copyright 2019 - All rights reserved.

The content contained within this book may not be reproduced, duplicated or transmitted without direct written permission from the author or the publisher.

Under no circumstances will any blame or legal responsibility be held against the publisher, or author, for any damages, reparation, or monetary loss due to the information contained within this book. Either directly or indirectly.

Legal Notice:

This book is copyright protected. This book is only for personal use. You cannot amend, distribute, sell, use, quote or paraphrase any part, or the content within this book, without the consent of the author or publisher.

Disclaimer Notice:

Please note the information contained within this document is for educational and entertainment purposes only. All effort has been executed to present accurate, up to date, and reliable, complete information. No warranties of any kind are declared or implied. Readers acknowledge that the author is not engaging in the rendering of legal, financial, medical or professional advice. The content within this book has been derived from various sources. Please consult a licensed professional before attempting any techniques outlined in this book.

By reading this document, the reader agrees that under no circumstances is the author responsible for any losses, direct or indirect, which are incurred as a result of the use of information contained within this document, including, but not limited to, — errors, omissions, or inaccuracies.

Table Of Contents

Chapter 1: Introduction to Machine Learning   6
- Machine Learning Evolution   7
- Artificial Intelligence   9
- Importance of Artificial Intelligence   9
- The Significance of Machine Learning in the Modern Business World   11
- Why Is Machine Learning so Important?   11

Chapter 2: Machine Learning Applications   13
- Business and other Applications of Machine Learning   13
- Machine Learning Methods in Use   15
- The Hype and Reality of Machine Learning   17
- Real Life Cases of Machine Learning in B2B Applications   18

Chapter 3: Machine Learning Over The Years   20
- Early History of Machine Learning   20
- Between the 1980's - 1990's   21
- The 21st Century   22
- Growth and Evolution of Artificial intelligence   23
- AI Will Replace Tasks Mostly, Not Jobs   24
- Winners and Losers Due to the Rise of AI   25
- Early Investors in Artificial Intelligence   26

Chapter 4: What are Neural Networks?   29
- Machine Learning, Deep Learning, and Neural Networks   29
- Building Neural Networks   30
- Training the Models   32
- Skills & Tools Required   33
- Human Brain vs. Neural Networks (Man vs. Machine)   34
- Use of Neurons   35
- About Artificial Neural Network   35

Biological Neural Network	36
Biological Network Learning	38
Learning for the Artificial Neural Networks	40
Widespread Exposure	41
Man versus Machine	43
Can Machine Learning Supersede the Human Brain?	44

Chapter 5: Twenty Real World Applications of Machine Learning	**47**
Managing Large Amount of Data	47
Machine Learning for Who?	48
Real-World Applications of Machine Learning	49
1. Virtual Voice-Activated Personal Assistants	50
2. Predictions During Commuting	51
3. Video Surveillance	51
4. Social Media	52
5. Malware & Email Spam Filtering	53
6. Online Customer Support	53
7. Refining Search Engine Results	54
8. Product Recommendations	54
9. Online Fraudulent Transactions Detection	55
10. Walking Talking (Humanoid) Robots Using Imitation Learning	55
11. Bioinformatics	55
12. Text and Hypertext Categorization	56
13. Stock Market Trading	56
14. Automatic Translation	57
15. Self-Driving Cars	57
16. Smart Computers	57
17. Spotify	58
18. Shadow Profiles	59
19. Biometrics	59
20. Self-Replicating Machines	60

Chapter 6: What is Predictive Analytics?	**61**
How Does Predictive Analytics Work?	61
Commonly Used Predictive Models	62

Classifiers 63
  Machine Learning and Predictive Analytics Applications 64
  Developing The Right Environment 65
  Predictive Models 65

Chapter 7: What is Data Mining? 67
  Data Mining Techniques 68

Chapter 8: How to Optimize your Business 71
  Step 1: Identifying What Needs To Be Optimized 72
  Step 2: Consider Automation 73
  Step 3: Adopting Technology and Total Process Change 74
  Step 4: Optimizing the Business Resources 75
  Step 5: Optimizing Business Operations 77
  Step 6: Performing Research to Predict Product Trends 80
  Step 7: Observing Patterns and Prediction. Differentiate between real trends and momentary crazes 82
  Step 8: Building a Data-Driven Strategy 83
  Step 9: Targeting and Connecting with Potential Customers 87

Chapter 9: Machine Learning Applications for Marketing 92
  1. Customer Segmentation and Discovery by Clustering 92
  2. Content Optimization by using Multi-Arm Contextual Bandits 93
  3. Regression Models with Dynamic Pricing 93
  4. Text Classification for Personalization and User Insight 93
  5. Text Extraction and Summary for Trending News 94
  6. Machine Translation Using Attentional Neural Networks 94
  7. Text Generation by using RNN (Recurrent Neural Networks) 94
  8. Dialog System for Chatbots and Automation of Customer Experience 95
  9. Voice Based Searching Using TTS and STT 95
  10. Brand Object Recognition by using Computer Vision 95
  11. Original Media with GANs (Generative Adversarial Networks) 96
  12. Automation of Robotic Processes for Marketing Operations 96
  13. Superior Reporting by Using Automated Data Visualization 97
  14. Sequential Marketing Decisions Using Reinforcement Learning 97

Chapter 10: Machine Learning Applications for Finance   98
    1. Portfolio Management   98
    2. Trading with Algorithms   99
    3. Detecting Frauds   99
    4. Insurance or Loan Underwriting   100
    5. Machine Learning and Cryptocurrencies   101
    6. Day Trading with Machine Learning   101

Chapter 11: The Future of AI and Machine Learning   103
    1. Better Unsupervised algorithms   103
    2. Improved Personalization   104
    3. Raised Use of Quantum Computing   104
    4. Enhanced Cognitive Services   105
    5. The Rise of Machines (Robots)   105
    6. Impact of ML/AI on Employment and Verticals   105

Chapter 12: Conclusion   107

Algorithm Example: Hotel Recommendation Engine Using Machine Learning   108

Algorithm Example: Customer Segmentation by using Clustering Algorithms   119

Chapter 1: Introduction to Machine Learning

Machine learning is one of the applications of AI (Artificial Intelligence). It provides various systems the capability to automatically learn and also improve from its experience despite not being explicitly programmed to do so. It focuses on the development of different computer programs which can access and use the data to learn by themselves. Machine learning is the concept of mathematical models and algorithms used by computer systems to progressively increase their output on specific tasks.

Machine learning is revolutionizing the computing world with its digital interactions because it is a form of AI. These interactions are made possible cheaply, quickly, and automatically, while also analyzing a massive amount of complex data. Machine learning is priceless and critical to several new applications and also to the ones planned in future. Machine learning empowers some innovative automated technologies such as facial recognition, recommended engines, fraud protection, and self-driven cars.

This process of learning for the computers begins with data or observations like instructions or direct experience and then look for patterns in the data that allow them to make better decisions in future based on the examples that have been provided. The main aim for machine learning is to allow the machine to learn automatically without any human assistance or intervention and learn to adjust things accordingly.

The term machine learning was coined in the year 1959 Arthur Samuel. However, it was Tom Mitchell who provided a more widely quoted and more formal definition of the various algorithms studied under the field of machine learning. This definition is: "A computer program is said to learn from experience E with respect to some class of tasks T and performance measure P if its performance at tasks in T, as measured by P, improves with experience E."

This definition basically offers a fundamental operational version of the term instead of defining it cognitively. Alan Turing proposed in his papers the query "Can machines think?" to be replaced by "Can machine do what we can do?". Humans can do certain things as thinking entities. The Turing proposal exposes the various characteristics that may be possessed by machines that think.

Allowing computers to learn from their experience requires the use of automation and data analysis of analytical models and algorithms. Machine learning empowers the machines to search and identify concealed insights without being automated to look for them when exposed to new data. Although the technology is not novel, it is gaining momentum as there are a number of things to learn and know about ML. The various factors responsible for the resurgent interest in machine learning are affordable computational processing, growing volumes of data sets and affordable storage options for data. Modern-day companies can make an educated decision by using machine learning algorithms as they uncover trends, patterns, and connections with minimal human interference.

Machine Learning Evolution

Machine learning in the modern world is different than what it used to be earlier. This is mainly due to the emergence of new technologies. In the past, the technology gained momentum due to pattern recognition and the fact that a computer did not have to be programmed to understand how to learn or work on a specific task. Imagine that, having a machine that already knows what to do next without you having to tell it anything.

Scientists were intrigued by this concept of artificial intelligence and began investigating further whether or not computers could learn from data. The focus was not on iterative learning, but more so on learning new things they did not already have information about. The computers began to adapt to the new data they were provided over a certain time period. They were able to make decisions based on similar past situations and patterns.

People these days are taking note of the fact that the machines are able to apply difficult mathematical calculations, such as handling large data, while also performing at a faster rate. Take for example, the Google self-driving car, which is built on machine learning principles. Another significant use of machine learning in our daily lives can be seen in the recommendations used by Amazon or Netflix. ML can also be pooled with the creation of linguistic rules. Twitter uses this, so you can see what customers are saying about you. Machine learning is even being used to detect fraud in various industrial sectors.

Gone are the days in which the programmers would tell the computer how to resolve an issue at hand. We have reached an era where the machines are left to resolve the issues on their own. They identify the pattern from each data set. Analyzing the hidden patterns and trends makes it simple to guess the future problems as well and also from them reoccurring. The machine learning algorithms normally follow a certain kind of data and they use the patterns in the data to answer the queries. For example, you show the machine a series of photographs of dogs and say "This is a dog." and later show some other photos saying "This is not a dog." Now if you show some photographs to the computer it will be trying to identify whether or not the photographs are that of a dog. However, every correct or incorrect guess made by the machine is stored in its memory. This makes the machine smarter in the long run and enriches its knowledge over a time period.

Artificial Intelligence

Artificial intelligence is also called machine intelligence. It is the intelligence displayed by the machines in contrast with the natural intelligence shown by the humans and other animals. It is the development of computer systems to be able to perform the tasks that need human intelligence like speech recognition, visual perception, translation between languages and decision making. The word artificial intelligence was coined in 1956 but has gained popularity nowadays due to advanced algorithms, increased data volumes, and improvement in storage and computing power. US defense took up this work proactively in the 1960s and began teaching computers to mimic human reasoning. The early work paved way for the formal reasoning used in the computers today. The artificial intelligence is responsible for some of the decision support systems along with smart systems that can be used augment human capabilities.

Importance of Artificial Intelligence

Artificial intelligence automates the discovery via data and repetitive learning. But, it is different from the robotic and hardware driven automation. Rather than automating manual tasks, it performs high volume, frequent and computerized tasks reliably without tiring. However, even for this kind of automation, the human inquiry is a must to set up the system and to ask the right questions.

By using neural networks, AI analyzes deeper and more data that has several layers. Creating a fraud detection system having five hidden layers was considered impossible a few years back. All this has changed now with computer power. The deep learning models need a lot of data as they learn from the data itself. More the data you feed the system more accurate it becomes.

AI has achieved great accuracy via deep neural networks which were considered impossible earlier. For example, your interaction with Google Search, Alexa and Google Photos is based on deep learning and they keep on becoming more accurate as we use them more. AI techniques are widely used in the medical field. These are image classification, object recognition, and deep learning. They can be used to find cancer in MRIs with the same accuracy as that of well-trained radiologists.

AI is responsible for adding intelligence to existing products. In many cases the AI will not be sold as an independent product rather the existing product will be improved with better capabilities similar to Siri which was added as a new feature to the Apple products. Many technologies at home and at the workplace can be improved by using conversational platforms, bots, smart machines and automation, for example, security intelligence or investment analysis.

The AI has adapted via progressive learning algorithms which allow data to do the programming. It finds regularities and structure in the data and as a result, a new skill is acquired. It becomes a predictor or a classifier. Now it can teach itself to play chess or what product to recommend the next time you are online. And the models adopt the new data provided. Another technique used by AI is back propagation which allows the machine to adjust via training and added data when the first time answer is not correct.

AI actually gets the most out of provided data. When the algorithms become self-learning, the data becomes an intellectual property. All answers are in the data. You need to apply the AI to pull them out. As the role of data becomes more important than ever it creates competitive advantage. In case you have the most useful data in an industry you will win despite everyone else applying the same technique.

The Significance of Machine Learning in the Modern Business World

Most organizations dealing in a large amount of data have realized the importance of machine learning. By using the hidden insight from this data the businesses can work more efficiently and can also acquire a competitive spirit. Apart from bringing about affordable and simple computational processing it also brings along cost-effective storage options, machine learning has made it feasible to create models that accurately and quickly process and analyze a massive amount of complex data. Along with making it possible for companies to analyze trends and patterns from a range of data sets, the ML is also capable of automating the analysis process. This used to be done by humans previously. The companies can now deliver personalized services along with differentiated products that cater to the various requirements of the clients accurately. ML is also helpful to the organizations in identifying opportunities that can be lucrative to them in the long run. When you are planning to create an effective machine learning system for increasing your business then here is what you need to do:

- Have knowledge of fundamental and advanced algorithms.
- Must possess great data preparation capabilities.
- Have scalability.
- Have knowledge of Ensemble Modeling.
- Be ready for iterative and automation processes.

Why Is Machine Learning so Important?

In order to understand the uses of ML, we can consider some of the examples in which machine learning is applied. Fraud detection, self-driving Google car and online recommendation engines such as Netflix and Facebook are some examples. Netflix showcases movies and shows you like and it helps you with suggestions when there are more items to consider or when you are trying to get yourself a little something from Amazon. They are all examples of applied machine learning. These examples echo the crucial role machine learning is playing in the modern world which is rich with data. Computers can help in filtering the useful pieces of information and can result in major advancements. We are already experiencing how useful and effective the technology is and it is being implemented in a range of industries.

With constant developments in the field, there has been a constant rise in demand, uses and the significance of machine learning. A large amount of data has become the prime buzzword in the last few years. It is primarily because of a high degree of sophistication achieved in the field of ML which allows you to analyze a large amount of data quickly. It has also changed the way data is extracted and interpreted. Generic methods are used for this purpose which use automatic sets to replace conventional statistical techniques.

Chapter 2: Machine Learning Applications

Business and other Applications of Machine Learning

The actual value of machine learning has been identified by the organizations across the world. This is especially true for the industries that deal in large amount of data. By using the insights obtained from the data these companies are able to leverage their efficiency along with controlling costs to get an edge over other organizations. Here is how some domains are implementing ML for better:

Sales and Marketing

Organizations use the machine learning techniques to analyze purchase history of their clients and make highly personalized recommendations for the next purchase of their products. This capability to collect, analyze and use client data in order to provide a personalized shopping scenario is the future of marketing and sales.

Government

Various government agencies such as public safety and utilities for example have the need for machine learning. These agencies have many data sources which can be mined to identify useful patterns and insights. As an example sensor data is analyzed to find the ways to minimize cost and raise efficiency. As we know the ML is useful in minimizing identity thefts and detect fraud.

Finance Services

There are organizations in finance sector that are able to identify some insights in the finance related data as well as stop any instances of finance related fraud by using the ML.

The ML technology can also be used to identify investment and trade opportunities. Use of internet oriented surveillance helps in locating individuals or institutions that are prone to financial risks. You can take necessary actions to prevent fraudulent transactions.

Healthcare Services

With the advancement of wearable sensors and instruments that use data to access a patient body in real time, the machine learning is becoming increasingly popular in healthcare. Sensors in the wearables provide real-time information like heartbeat, blood pressure, overall health condition, and other crucial parameters. Medical experts and doctors can use this information to analyze health condition of individuals, create a pattern from their history and predict the re-occurrence of the ailment in future. This ML technology also aids the medical experts to analyze data to identify various trends that enable better diagnosis and treatment.

Oil & Gas

Oil and gas industry needs the machine learning technology the most. It can be used for analyzing the underground minerals and locating new energy resources to stream oil distribution. The ML applications for this industry are great and are expanding even today.

Transport

By using the travel history and patterns of travelling on different routes, ML can aid different organizations predict potential issues that may rise on different routes. The transportation people can advise their clients to opt for alternative routes in such cases. The transport companies and delivery services are increasingly using the ML technology to carry out the data analysis and modeling to make educated decisions and help the clients make smart decisions when they are using their services for travel.

Machine Learning Methods in Use

Even though there are two more widely used machine learning methods called supervised and unsupervised learning in business use, there are some other in existence as well. Here is an overview of some commonly used and accepted machine learning methods:

1. Supervised Learning

The algorithms, in this case, are trained by using labeled examples in various scenarios as the input. And in this case, the desired output is already available. A machine, for example, could have data points called F and R where F stands for "Failed" and R stands for "Running". The learning algorithm will receive a set of instructions as input along with their corresponding correct outputs. The learning algorithm will in such case compare the real outcome with the correct output and will flag an error in case there is a discrepancy. By using different methods like classification, regression, prediction, and gradient boosting the supervised learning algorithm uses various patterns to proactively guess events or predict values of labels on the additional unlabeled data. This method of ML is used commonly in cases where historical data is to be used to predict values or events that are likely to occur in the future. You can take the example of a credit card. You can expect when a card transaction is likely to be a fraud or predict which clients of your insurance company are likely to file the claims.

2. Unsupervised Learning

In this kind of machine learning the application is found in sectors where the data has no historical labels. In this case, the system is not given the right output answer and the algorithm is required to recognize what is being inputted. The main idea here is to analyze data and locate a pattern and structure within the data set. The transactional data serves as a quality source for a data set for unsupervised learning. For example, this kind of algorithm identifies the customer details having similar attributes and allows the businesses to treat them usefully in their marketing campaigns. Likewise, the algorithm can also recognize the features that differentiate customer details from one another. In either case, it is all about identifying similar structures in the available set of data. Apart from this, these algorithms can recognize outliers from the available sets of data. The most commonly used techniques for unsupervised learning are:

- Self-organizing maps.
- K-means clustering.
- Mapping of nearest neighbors.
- Value Decomposition.

3. Semi-supervised Learning

The semi-supervised learning is utilized and applied in a similar scenario to the one that is applied in supervised learning technique. But the difference is that it uses both labeled and unlabeled data for the training. Ideally, a small labeled data coupled with large volumes of unlabeled data is utilized. This is because it takes less time, energy and money to get unlabeled data. This kind of machine learning is normally used with methods such as regression, prediction, and classification. Organizations that find it difficult to meet the high costs that you associate with the labeled learning methods goes for the semi-supervised learning techniques.

4. Reinforcement Learning

Reinforcement learning is mainly used in robotics, gaming, and navigation. The actions that will get the best rewards are recognized by the algorithms by using trial and error method. There are three main types of reinforcement learning viz. agent, action and the environment. The agent, of course, is the decision maker, the action is what the agent does and lastly, the environment is the thing the agent interacts with. The idea behind this kind of learning is selecting actions that amplify the rewards within a specific time period. By following the right policies the agent can achieve his target quicker. So the main aim for reinforcement learning is to recognize the best way or method for helping the business achieve their goals quicker. Although the humans are capable of creating some good models within a week, the ML can develop thousands of these models within the same time period.

The Hype and Reality of Machine Learning

There are a lot of myths involved when you are answering the question, "How does machine learning work?" There are many things believed such as it learns automatically and that it doesn't need any customization or modifications from the companies using it. It is also believed that it can fit any business scenario and can solve all problems. Let's see which of these beliefs are true. Similar to any other technology never settle for anything less than real machine learning. As various industries are realizing the transformational value of Artificial Intelligence and machine learning, they are realizing the need to manage huge content. The demand for ML-based solutions is increasing but not all ML-based solutions are equally useful. They need to be flexible, fast, powerful and above all intelligent.

Like in case of any other technology ML has a great potential for businesses but in some cases and not always. Despite the myths and the hype generated ML might not always be the right solution for analyzing structured data. But it is a different method of programming a machine to execute tasks. So it is significant to have the right expectations about the use of ML for businesses. You need to remember that there is nothing magic about ML.

Machine learning is not exactly like human intelligence as it is a technology that learns via training and procedures used for specific inputs in order to apply the text analysis approach. ML does not have any embedded knowledge. It requires a set of data for its training. This means a lot of manual work is required in most cases.

Also, there are limitations to the number of improvements that are possible and it is difficult to figure out whether the system has improved or whether you need to improve it further. Although the level of accuracy reached is high, things could be better. There is little room for the discovery of errors as you are required to go back to square one in such a case.

Real Life Cases of Machine Learning in B2B Applications

It has to be said that machine learning is not a magic thing. However, it has the potential to serve as a strong extender of human cognition. This capability is particularly useful in B2B and B2C types of businesses. It proves to be useful in identifying patterns in a large number of users and customer data helping improve the company performance. It is helpful in many areas such as a more influential content creation, saved marketing costs and a huge number of paid clients. Let's see some applications developed by vendors and find out how they are being used by the B2B companies to drive business decisions and have better reach to serve their clients.

1. GlaxoSmithKline

GlaxoSmithKline is a global healthcare organization that makes and develops healthcare products and pharmaceuticals. It uses the natural language and text analytics technology by Luminoso as a non-invasive solution for obtaining insight into the growing concerns of parents about vaccinations. The company applied algorithms for sifting through and teasing out patterns of parental fears including possible links between autism and vaccination. This could have been the primary driver to avoid vaccination. The premium healthcare company used detailed insights to help create some informational content that particularly addressed this concern by the parents and provided an incentive for the follow through with early childhood vaccination.

Wargaming

Wargaming is big in the gaming industry. It used the advanced analytics platform by Cloudera as a solution to process more than 500 million daily events. This is massive and equivalent to 3 TB raw data. This enabled real-time recommendations for engaging the users better and present relevant attractive offers. An extremely smart and solid infrastructure permitted Wargaming to increase their campaign 10 fold and in the end resulted in raising the customer response by three times.

Zendesk

By now ZenDesk has become one of the most popular CRM platforms in the sales and services field. It was looking for a mechanical solution to target their audience better. They felt that the audience ready to purchase their products was too broad and led to excessive costs for the PPC (Pay Per Click) and SEM (Search Engine Marketing) leads. They used MarainalQ's platform for social media engagement and soon they were able to identify patterns in the contact information data. They used it to create categories of different personas. The company says it led to the lead volume growing by 4 times and as a result drove the cost-per-lead down.

Chapter 3: Machine Learning Over The Years

Early History of Machine Learning

The first cases of neural network were established in 1943 when Warren McCulloch an established neurophysiologist and another mathematician called Walter Pitts wrote a paper about neurons and it talked about how they work. They together decided to create a model of their findings by using electrical circuits and in this manner, the first neural networks were born.

The world famous Turing test was created by Alan Turing in the year 1950. The test is pretty simple. For a machine to pass the test it has to convince a human that it is a human and not a machine. It was 1952 when the first computer program came into existence which was able to learn as it ran. Arthur Samuel created the game which played checkers. The very first artificial neural network was designed in 1958 by Frank Rosenblatt and it was called Perception. The main goal of the network was shape and pattern recognition.

Another instance of early neural networks can be located in 1959 when Marcian Hoff and Bernard Widrow created two models at Stanford University. First of them was called ADELINE and it was capable of detecting binary patterns. That is in a stream of bits it was able to predict which the next one will be. Its next generation was called MADELINE and it was capable of eliminating echo from the phone lines. As it had a real-world application it is in use even today.

In spite of the success of MADELINE, there wasn't much progress until the late 1970s for several reasons. But the main reason was the popularity of Von Neumann architecture. In this architecture data and instructions are stored in the same memory. It is relatively easier to understand than compared to neural networks and as a result, several people developed programs based on it.

Between the 1980's - 1990's

It was in 1982 when the interest in the neural networks started picking up again. During the year John Hopfield suggested the creation of a network that has bidirectional lines which were similar to how the neutrons work. In addition to this, Japan announced that they will be focusing more on the advanced neural networks. This pushed the Americans into funding the field and as a result, more research was conducted in the area.

The neural networks make use of back propagation and this important development happened in the year 1986. Three researchers from the Stanford psychology department thought about extending an algorithm made by Hoff and Widrow in 1962. The development led to allowing the use of multiple layers in neural networks and thereby the creation of what is now known as "slow learners". They learn over a period of time.

There were not many developments in the area during the 1980s and 1990s. However, in the year 1997, Deep Blue an IBM computer which was a chess player beat the world chess champion. Since this development, there have been several more developments in the area such as in 1998. During a research at AT&T Bell Laboratories, digital recognition resulted in great accuracy while detecting handwritten postcodes of US Postal Service. The research used back propagation.

The 21st Century

At the beginning of the 21st century, several businesses realized the calculation potential of machine learning. Because of this reason, they started investing in research and they are trying to stay ahead of the rest of the field in the process. Some of the larger projects in machine learning include:

- **AlexNet in 2012** - It won the ImageNet competition with a huge margin in the year 2012. This led to the use of convolutional neural networks and GPUs in machine learning. They were also responsible for the creation of the activation function ReLU which is capable of improving the efficiency of the CNNs.
- **GoogleBrain in 2012** - It was a deep neural network and was created by Google's Jeff Dean. It focused on pattern recognition in videos and images. This network was able to utilize Google's resources and as a result, it was incomparable to other smaller neural networks. Later it was used to detect the objects in the YouTube videos.
- **DeepMind in 2014** - The Company was later bought by Google. It can play fundamental video games at the same level as that of humans. It managed to beat a professional in the year 2016 at a game called Go which is considered as one of the most difficult board games in the world.
- **DeepFace in 2014** - FaceBook created this deep neural network which they claimed is capable of recognizing people with the same accuracy as any human.
- **Amazon Machine Learning Platform in 2015** - It is a part of Amazon's web services and aptly displays how big organizations are getting involved in machine learning. They say that it drives several of their internal systems from Alexa and search recommendations to more experimental services such as Amazon Go and Prime Air.
- **Open AI in 2015** - It is a non-profit institution which was created by Elon Musk and some other people. It was created to see If artificial intelligence is useful to benefit humanity.
- **ResNet in 2015** - It was a major advancement in CNN architectures.

- **U-Net in 2015** - It specializes in the field of biomedical image segmentation and comes with a CNN architecture. It introduced equal amounts of upsampling and downsampling layers and was able to skip connections as well.

Growth and Evolution of Artificial intelligence

Well the artificial intelligence is coming of age and it can be termed as a beginning of real autonomy. It is expected that within the next 4 years the AI industry growth will explode and it will start making a real impact on modern society and businesses. By the end of the 2010s, it is believed that the recent quick advances in the field of AI will plant their feet firmly and progress into the AGI phase. This will be true autonomy. The machines and software powered by AI are likely to replace human supervision. They will embark on their destined path of sentient beings. This will happen in the distant future though and is not likely to take place soon. However, the AI growth will start hitting the roof and it will start influencing society and businesses.

The global AI industry was at $5 Billion in the marketplace by revenue in the year 2015. This is a good size for a developing sector. It is expected that by 2020 exponential improvements and greater adoption will lead to its doubling the revenue at least to become a $12.5 Billion industry. This makes for approximately 20% annual growth rate if we assume that the company values increase in the multiples of 10 to 15x which is at par with other similar emerging and fast-growing industries in the technology area. Artificial Intelligence as a standalone sector has the capability to claim a market cap of 120 to 180 billion USD by the year 2020.

The software companies will, of course, take up the baton and forge ahead thereby pushing the borders of automation, searching and social media. AI is also dubbed as a machine's brain and it is likely to automate sectors such as automobile and unmanned drones. The AI software will create lots of business opportunities and social value. For example, the chatbots or virtual assistants will offer expert advice and assistance. The smart robots will act as robotic advisors in the field of insurance, finance, media, legal and journalism. They will provide instant research and findings and within the healthcare sector the AI developed software will help in diagnosis and aid. Other benefits it offers are improved efficiency in the R&D projects by decreasing the time required for marketing, optimization of transport and hoarding chain networks. It will also improve governance with a better decision making process.

Even today you can find expert systems that can share and scan overviews of legal documents collected from distant or obscure earlier court rulings within seconds. It will help lawyers save time and money. Independent driving is still in its hibernation stage but it has made great progress. Some self-driven taxis were recently made available in Singapore. The list goes on thereby providing an inevitable entry and domination of AI in the everyday lives.

So are we taking the risk of being replaced? Well, these advances in technology are bound to come at a price. Unemployment in the field of technology is a byproduct of the progress. It is a known fact that mechanical looms sent the artisan weavers to paucity. Innovation of the tractor pushed millions of people out of jobs and robotics sliced numerous workers in all kind of manufacturing. The rising integration of AI is going to yield better productivity in near future but the result of this is cull in the employment area.

AI Will Replace Tasks Mostly, Not Jobs

The concerns expressed over the advancement are legitimate. However, AI will not develop to such a scale that its extensive adoption will activate mass layoffs. Other technology will still be utilized in some niche applications and will not achieve the critical level that will threaten employment at a global level. Remember, in most cases, the AI is about to take over the tasks and not the jobs. But employment on a global scale will not escape unscathed. Due to the automation of the tasks which rely on subtle judgment, problem-solving skills and analysis the AI will become a threat to the predictable, low-skill and routine jobs, especially in the retail and financial services sectors. It will also affect automobile and other manufacturing units in case of broader automation.

At this stage, it is difficult to predict the exact impact of automation but if we assume 5% of jobs are routine in nature. It is expected that 2% of the worldwide jobs meaning around 50 to 75 million jobs worldwide will be affected. This is a significant number but pales in comparison to what opportunities AI will create. The rise and the following surge of AI will raise productivity and bring many opportunities for the workforce to upgrade their skill set and focus on the creative part.

Due to the emergence of AI other disruptive businesses such as apps or shared economies are likely to develop especially in the post-AI era. There will be an increased scope for employment which requires a greater level of personalization, craftsmanship, and creativity. These tasks will still need people to perform. It is difficult to imagine these tasks to be performed by humans at this time and so the high level of anxiety as a result with the AI integration. However, these will quell soon as new specializations will be required. This is similar to the industrial revolution which brought a boom for the factory workers.

Winners and Losers Due to the Rise of AI

AI will not only decrease costs with the automation of processes but it will also maximize revenues by providing help to marketers to introduce new products and services. Because of the limited size of the current market, it is believed that the direct beneficiaries at the moment are software companies and the robotics process automation sector. They will have the first mover's advantage. In the medium run, the AI industry will consolidate due to the several startups focused on using AI. But as the industry standards emerge slowly there will be winners and losers.

There will be some indirect beneficiaries such as hi-tech engineering and healthcare and some selected companies providing services due to improved efficiency in R & D. For example, AI can reduce costs by using predictive analytics and deep learning tools. Costs are significantly reduced by AI in the drug manufacturing organizations along with the time required for the production. It will predict the therapeutic use of new drugs thereby giving huge gains in terms of efficiency.

Where there are winners there are bound to be losers. Without adapting to the changing scenario the retail and automobile industries are likely to fall behind. As indicated earlier, the rise of AI will have a solid effect on certain sectors and the industries belonging to these areas will either finish or survive depending on the rapid changes in technology.

Early Investors in Artificial Intelligence

If the Bank of America dictum is to be adhered to, an early adoption is a key to a comparative advantage. Those who fail in making the right investment will see the competitive edge slip. Leading tech organizations such as IBM, Microsoft, Google, and Apple are scaling up their investment in AI.

IBM is currently involved in Watson which is a technology platform making use of natural language processing along with machine learning to reveal the insight from a massive amount of unstructured data. The IBM's Watson is being utilized to diagnose different diseases, analyze books and records and run college courses. Now, KPMG LLP and IBM are working together to provide cognitively powered insight into a huge volume of auditing and similar knowledge data with the empowerment of Watson.

Apple is known to be extremely secretive about their projects and acquisitions. But it is known that they are buying some AI startups. One such buy was Siri in the year 2010 which is now a part of their range. A more recent buy was Turi at approximately $200 million. It has several features, algorithms, services, and platforms thereby offering tremendous potential for being used in Apple's different applications and product range.

Recently NVIDIA and Baidu combined forces to use Artificial Intelligence in the creation of autonomous car platform for universal car manufacturers. A report from IHS incorporated suggests that the shipments of AI systems used in advanced driving assistance systems (ADAS) and in infotainment are expected to rise from 7 million in 2015 to a whopping 122 million by the year 2025. It is assessed that about 8% of new cars made use of AI-based platforms (with a majority focusing only on voice recognition) in 2015 the number is expected to rise to 100% by 2025 with several AI systems being installed in the vehicles.

Salesforce introduced Salesforce Einstein in some other developments. It integrates advanced AI possibilities in its core platform service making its CRM (Customer Relationship Management) a lot smarter. At the same time, Microsoft has recently created their AI arm called Microsoft AI and Research Group in order to accelerate the provision of the latest AI capabilities to the clients across apps, agents, infrastructure and services. Amazon, Google/DeepMind, IBM, Facebook, and Microsoft have together announced the creation of "Partnership on AI". It comes with a clear objective to address challenges and opportunities associated with AI technologies to aid people and society.

Google is the pioneer in AI and is actively focusing on machine learning algorithms and AI for several of its projects. Some of them include the self-driven cars, e-commerce, gaming, search engines, spam-email blocking by Gmail with its app assistant. AlphaGo was developed by Google/DeepMind and is working on health-related projects.

Different applications based on artificial intelligence are becoming popular in various sectors such as homes, hospitals, schools and certain industries but its adoption is raising some eyebrows as well. Social concerns such as privacy issues and unemployment are being raised. While robotics and AI technologies will raise the quality of life for humans and open new horizons, it will also shrink the job market by some distance.

The Bank of America is expecting the current AI and robot solutions market to rise to $153 billion by the year 2020 with around $70 billion for the AI based analytics and 83 billion for robotics. They are also saying that these technologies will yield $14-33 trillion as an economic impact by the year 2025 via gained efficiency and cost reduction. By adopting these technologies a potential boost of 30% in productivity across several industries can be observed and the labor costs can be cut down by around 25% at an average.

All-in-all the future of AI-based technologies will be decided by the weight of its benefits against the risks involved and the costs the technologies will incur. The technology giants are already deep into it and are ready to become a part and parcel of the transformation.

Chapter 4: What are Neural Networks?

We are all aware that the computers are better than humans at analyzing a series of numbers. However, what about the tasks which are more complex? How would you teach a computer what a cat seems to like or how to play a complex strategy game or even how to drive a car? Can it make predictions regarding the stock market? These are some of the more difficult tasks involving artificial intelligence and they are far more complex for the capabilities of machine learning and artificial intelligence. In these cases, the scientists go to neural networks for help.

The thing that sets neural networks to one side from the other ML algorithms in a wide range of industries and disciplines. Let's cut through the buzzwords and look at what the neural networks actually are and how they are different than other machine learning algorithms and how they are applied in modern scenarios.

Machine Learning, Deep Learning, and Neural Networks

Let's define these terms first. Machine learning we have defined and explained before in the earlier text. Let's look at deep learning and neural network. These are buzzwords in the technology world and they often get labeled as being one and the same. Although in reality, they are all related there are differences which are significant.

Machine Learning

Machine learning is a branch of computers that are related to building algorithms and it is guided by data. Instead of relying on human programmers to supply explicit directions the machine learning algorithms make use of training sets consisting of real-world data to create models which are more sophisticated and accurate than humans could ever create on their own.

Neural Networks

Neural networks are a part of machine learning. They are subsets of algorithms built on the model of artificial neurons which is spread across 3 or more layers. However, there are other machine learning techniques which do not rely on neural networks.

Deep Learning

Within the neural networks there is a term called deep learning which is used for describing more complex networks with several layers than normal. The benefit of the added layers is that these networks are capable of developing higher levels of abstraction which is needed for some complex tasks such as automatic translation and image recognition.

Building Neural Networks

This concept of underpinning a neural network has been here for many decades. However, during the recent times its computing capability has caught up with the requirement. Distributed systems such as Hadoop's MapReduce paradigm clearly means that there is no need for a supercomputer to handle large computations. Neural networks need you to spread the work item across the clusters of cheap hardware.

The neural networks are well-equipped to identify non-linear patterns in a set data where there is no direct or one-to-one relationship between input and output figures. The network instead identifies the pattern between different combinations of inputs and outputs. Let us say that you are building a system that differentiates between different types of animals such as dogs, dolphins, lizards, cats based on the presence or absence of different features. So, in case of a sample, the presence of warm blood or four legs is not enough to clearly identify the animal as a dog or a cat as the same criteria are true for a lizard as well. Warm blood will also describe a dolphin but the presence of four legs as a criteria brings things closer to identifying the animal as a dog. If you multiply the number of labels and features by a million or even a few thousands you will have an idea about how these things work.

There have been many reports in the media suggesting artificial neural networks working like a human brain but in reality they are being too simplistic. For one there is a massive difference in scale. Although the neural networks have increased a great deal in size they still consist of a few million neurons. This pales into insignificance compared to the huge 85 billion neurons present in any normal human brain.

The other major difference in the two lies in how the neurons are connected. Inside a human brain all the neurons are connected to several neurons close by. In a typical neural network the information flows only in one direction. In neural networks the information is spread across 3 layers:

- **Input Layer:** The input layer contains neurons that only perform the function of receiving and passing on the data. The number of neurons inside the input layer will be equal to the features in the data set.
- **Outside Layer:** The outside layer contains a number of nodes which depends on the kind of model you are building. For a classification system there will be a single

node for every type of label you are applying. Similarly there will be a single node which puts out a value for a regression system.

- **Hidden Layer:** Between these two layers the things start to get more interesting as there lies what is called as a hidden layer. It contains a number of neurons. How many neurons it contains will depend on the number present in the input and output layers. These nodes in the hidden layer will apply transformers to the input before passing it on. As this network gets training these nodes become more predictive and accurate and the output begins to get more weight.

Training the Models

One of the ways of thinking of neural networks is by imagining a black box having several knobs on its side. Yann LeCun who is a pioneer of neural networks describes them this way. Let's take the example of a neural network in which we are trying to train the network to predict whether a picture is that of a cat or not. This is a real-life example. Training a model involves fiddling with these knobs until the output layer can accurately identify a cat's picture. It comes without saying that when many knobs are involved it is not possible to turn them all manually. This is where the sophisticated machine learning algorithm comes in. The algorithms adjust these knobs automatically until the model fits the input data. This means they are adjusting the weighing functions of different neurons in the hidden layers.

Another important thing to take into consideration is, similar to this example we are adjusting the knobs until we have one great dog detector or we could tweak them a little until there is a great cat detector. Or we can re-adjust the knobs until we have one great big submarine detector. The point to the discussion is that the structures are generalized meaning that the same fundamental structures can be trained to reply to a number of queries. This is the reason why neural networks are more powerful. The key to the whole thing is in what machine learning algorithms and weighing functions we employ.

Skills & Tools Required

Neural networks add a cutting edge to the machine language technology and also artificial intelligence. Implementing this technology needs expertise in statistical analysis, large data processing, distributed systems, and other related fields. Luckily there are a lot of libraries available which make designing and implementing the neural networks relatively simple. Here are the more popular options:

TensorFlow

It is a high profile entry in the field of machine learning and is developed by Google as an open-source successor to the DistBelief which was their former framework for training the neural network. This framework makes use of a system of nodes which is multi-layered to allow you to set up quickly, train, and install artificial neural networks by using huge datasets. This allows Google to find objects in photographs or understand the words in their voice recognition app.

Scikit-learn

It builds on the foundational Python libraries such as SciPy and NumPy by adding a set of algorithms required for the common data mining and machine learning tasks. These include support for supervised and unsupervised neural networks both. Scikit-learn as a library has a lot of things going for it. It has tools which are well documented and its contributions are prepared by several ML experts. Significantly it is a curated library meaning, the developers don't have to select between various versions of the algorithm. The ease of use and power of the option makes it popular among many of data-heavy startups including OKCupid, Birchbox, Spotify, and EverNote.

Theano

This is a machine learning library from Python that makes use of syntax similar to that of NumPy to evaluate and optimize mathematical expressions. What sets it apart is the use of the machine GPU to make data-intensive calculations that are 100x quicker than the CPU. The speed of Theano makes it extremely valuable for the deep learning other complex computational tasks.

DeepLearning4j

This is a Java-based library used for implementing neural networks that are widely used for anomaly detection, recommender systems, and image recognition. It comes with APIs which allows the software to be used with the more data-oriented languages such as Python, Clojure, and Scala.

Human Brain vs. Neural Networks (Man vs. Machine)

The capability of learning is often considered as the hallmark of human intelligent life. Machine learning has now developed the capability to learn and extrapolate information out of data sets to accomplish difficult tasks such as classifying previously unknown occurrences. There is a striking similarity between how the machines learn and how we humans think and there are significant differences as well. We can definitely build a secure atmosphere by comparing and contrasting the biological learning with machine learning or artificial intelligence.

Use of Neurons

In case of biological neural networks, the learning emerges out of interconnections between ranges of neurons present inside the brain. These interconnections of neurons change the configurations as the brain is exposed to different stimuli. The changes include new connections, strengthening of existing connections and disposing of unwanted connections. For example, if a person repeats a task repeatedly the stronger the neurological connection will be until the task is learned.

Now the neurons can process further stimuli by using the earlier ones for the reference. The neurons along with these pre-established recommendations from its memory along with perceptions based on activation of some neurons will process the stimuli. For every stimulus, a different subset from a huge pool of neurons gets activated during the cognition. This incredible design from biology has led to the inspiration for data scientists to design artificial intelligence. The **artificial neural networks** are also known as **ANNs** are trying to mimic this behavior in an abstract to a smaller and easier scale.

About Artificial Neural Network

The ANN consists of layers of interconnected neurons which receive a set of inputs along with a set of weights. Then they perform mathematical manipulations and output results are obtained out of a set of activations which are identical to the synopses of the biological neurons. Although the ANNs are typically hundreds or thousands in numbers, the biological neural network working in the human brain consists of billions of neurons. At a high level the neural network consists of 4 components:

1. Neurons
2. Weights
3. Topology -The interconnecting path between different neurons
4. The learning algorithm

Every one of this components differs drastically between the artificial neural network of the artificial intelligence software and the biological neural network belonging to the human brain. See below for the visualization of the human biological neuron.

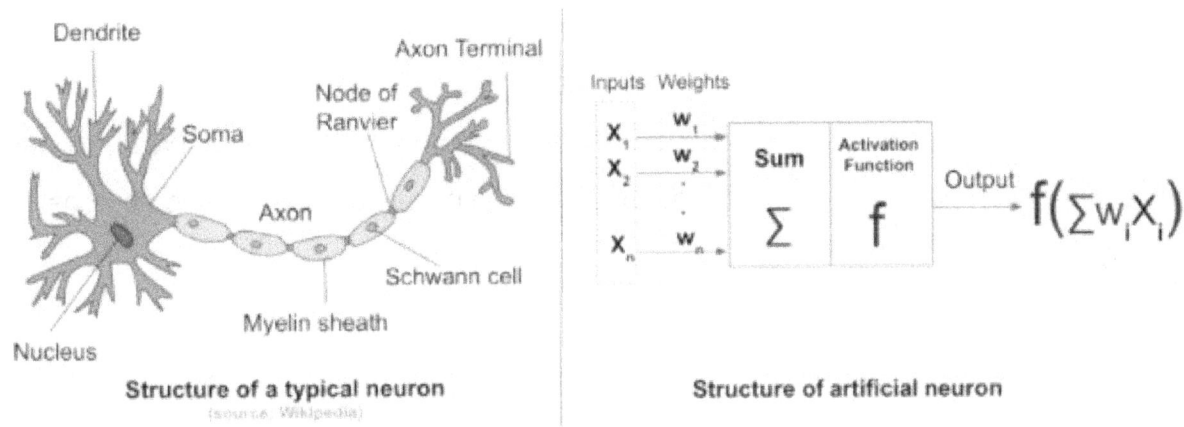

Figure 1: Visualization of the human biological neuron

Biological Neural Network

The biological neurons are depicted in the figure above. They contain a cell nucleus that receives input from the other neurons via a web of input branches or terminals called as dendrites. The blending of dendrites is referred to as a dendritic tree and it receives inhibitory or excitatory signals from other neurons through electrochemical exchange with neurotransmitters.

The number of input signals to reach the cellular nucleus depends on the volume of action potentials propagating from earlier neurons and the conductivity of ion channels feeding dendrites. These ion channels are responsible for the electric signal flow passing through neuron membrane.

Input signals of larger magnitude or more frequent signals normally result in better conductivity in ion channels or simpler signal propagation. Relying on this signal collected from all synapses of the dendritic tree the neurons are either inhibited or activated. In other words, they are either switched ON or OFF after a process termed as a neural summation. Neurons have an electrochemical threshold which is analogous to one activation function in the artificial neural networks. This governs whether the collected data is sufficient for activating the neurons. After this, the final results are fed to the other neurons and the process repeats. Here is a simple schematic figure depicting plausible neuronal topologies inside the human brain. Make note of the exciting large potential for loops and neurons feeding one another.

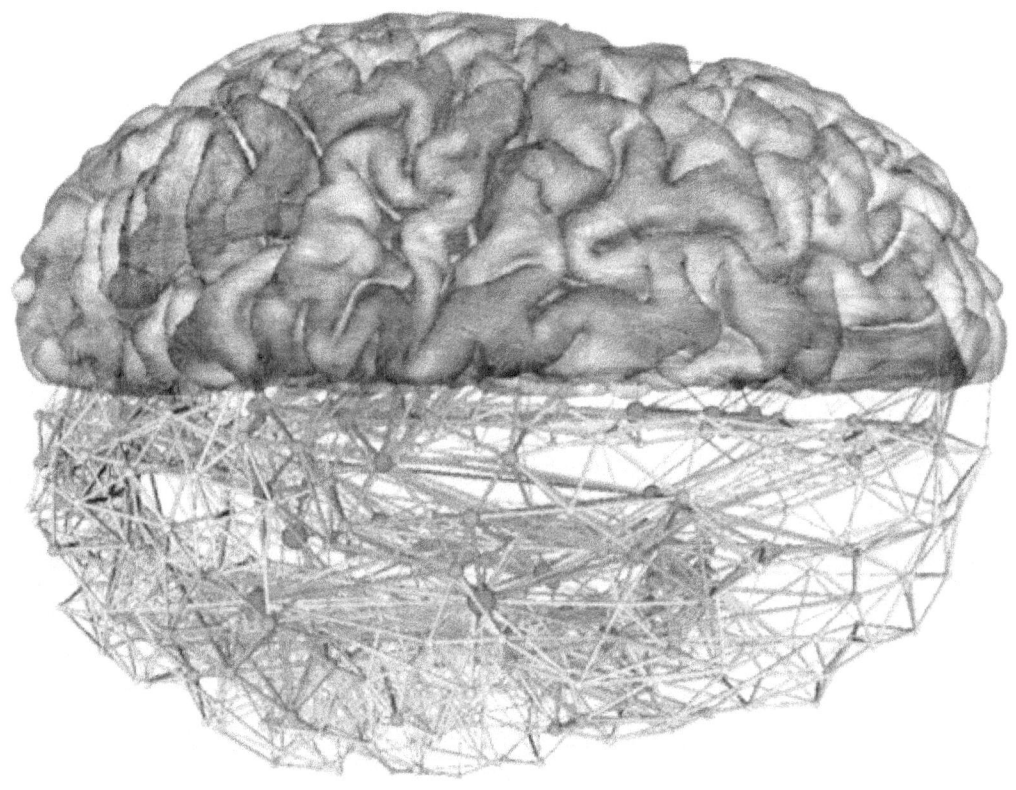

Figure 2: schematic figure depicting plausible neuronal topologies inside the human brain

Biological Network Learning

The biological neural networks, like that inside a human brain, learn by making small tweaks to existing representations. Its configuration contains a lot of significant information before it learns any new things. The strength of the connection between neurons or weights does not start randomly nor does the connection structure that is, in other words, the network topology. The initial state is in a portion genetically derived and it is a byproduct of its evolution.

Over a period of time, the biological networks learn to perform new functions by adjusting weights and topology both. The very fact that there is an initial representation which works well with several tasks is supported by the research. The study also suggests that the young one-month-old newborns are capable of recognizing faces. It is demonstrated by their learning to make a difference between other people and their parents. In other words, the concept of human face recognition has been passed down genetically from parents to the child.

As the babies progress and develop through their adolescence, childhood, adult life and through to the old age, they need to have the ability of facial recognition as they will see and meet new people and will need to get acquainted with them and must learn what they looked like. This within the biological networks is achieved by making alterations to the neural networks present in the human brain.

This same phenomenon applies to some other tasks as well including the passive tasks and those such as recognition of generic objects. Other such examples of active tasks like speech and movement include processing sound recognition by identifying the speech patterns. Learning these tasks is a gradual process and progressively small tweaks are employed to refine them later. The exact topologies are a function of the kind of stimuli on which the biological neural networks base their training.

One great example of this is "monocular deprivation studies" conducted by Torsten Wiesel and David Hubel. This study involves forcing an animal eye shut for a period of two months while it is in development and observing changes in their primary visual cortex. Results of the study showed that the cells which were generally responsive to the input from both the eyes suddenly were not receptive anymore. The cells in the brain and the cells in the eyes had both changed as a result of the experiment. The phenomenon is applicable to the humans as well. For example, the psychometric tests conducted on visual perception indicate that people who spend much of their lives in cities tend to be more receptive to sharp gradients and parallel lines than people from rural backgrounds. The rural people are more receptive to smooth texture gradients. This is more due to the overabundance of parallel structures available to the eye on the roads such as skyscrapers and windows.

Learning for the Artificial Neural Networks

The artificial neural networks, unlike their biological counterparts, are normally trained from scratch by using a fixed topology selected for the problem at hand. At the moment these topologies do not change over a period of time and weights get randomly adjusted and initialized through optimum algorithms to map aggregation of input stimuli to desired output functions. But the ANNs can learn from pre-existing representation as well. The process is called fine-tuning and means adjusting weights from a previously trained neural network topology at a slower learning rate. This is so in order to perform better on the newly supplied input training information.

It is easily possible to replicate the human brain but there is still a while to go before the human brain can be duplicated. Whether you are training from scratch or just performing the fine-tuning the update of weights procedure starts with the passage of data via the neural network, measurement of outcome and modification of weights accordingly. This together is how the artificial neural network learns. The weights are slowly propelled in the direction that improves the performance of the desired tasks such as raising recognition accuracy in the input pieces.

This kind of learning can be compared to that of a child trying to identify the usual objects or learning how to identify those objects. After several failed attempts and getting feedback on those about the accuracy, the child will make other attempts in another direction to get the correct response. The ANN performs the same tasks when it is learning. It is supplied stimuli which have known responses and the learning regime makes suitable adjustments so that the number of accurate answers increases and as a result the probability of a more precise output increases.

After the learning process is finished both the ANN and the child can make use of the previous representations of the issue to provide responses to the latest stimuli that have not been provided previously during the learning process. The child always learns through exposure to several problems, as many as possible. More the child practices solving the problem the better and faster it gets at solving the issues. This is because the relevant neurons in the child's brain become more defined. ANNs are similar to this. If they also have a great exposure to a wide distribution of stimuli for the specific tasks the more they will learn and they will respond better to newer stimuli from the same distribution that they were exposed to previously.

Widespread Exposure

It is a well-known fact that the more children are exposed to the experience of the world the more they learn even though this learning is painful at times. As a matter of fact when the learning is painful it serves as a sharp and additional feedback mechanism. In the same manner exposing an ANN to a range of stimuli in a certain domain is vital to training or fine tuning the neural network of any sort. It also ensures that you are not over fitting a model with just the one kind of stimuli.

With the increased representation of any specific kind of stimuli, the better the neural network becomes at classifying the new stimuli or generalizing a concept. This holds good for both biological and artificial neural networks. However, the biological neural networks are much better at the generalizing than their artificial counterparts. This happens partly because they are exposed to far more kinds of information and modalities because of their more advanced biological topology and learning algorithms. And the Darwinism plays a great part in it as well.

A good example of this is in the Black Swan Theory created by Nassim Taleb. This terminology comes from the common expressions from 16th century London. It stated that all swans are white because there has been no evidence of a swan of any other color. So a swan needs to be white to be classified as being from the same species. A Dutch explorer called Willem De Vlamingh, later on, witnessed black colored swans in Western Australia thereby changing the tight classification. The idea, in this case, is that if anyone grows seeing just the white swans his neural network is trained only with the distribution which says all swans are white. And if it is presented with a black swan it may not be able to classify the bird like a swan. This is because it has never seen the black swan before. If a person has grown up seeing both colored swans then he is in a better position to identify the swan type because of a biological neural network that is trained on the bigger distribution of swan types. It will have better knowledge of the many attributes that are associated with different kinds of swans.

The capability to extract and abstract knowledge from what has happened beforehand is called as a generalization and it is an extremely useful capability. It allows problem-solving in several domains faster with small weight adjustments. This process is regarded as fine tuning and it is the solution offered by the neural networks to transfer learning along with domain adaptation issues. Not many neuronal connections need re-wiring and this fact is the reason why average skiers are faster to pick up the snowboarding than the first-timers. This is also the reason why an artificial neural network which is trained for object detection and then fine-tuned for facial recognition will arrive at the right solution more than the one that is trained from scratch on the same data set as that used for face recognition.

Man versus Machine

It has to be accepted that the artificial neural networks we see today are still in the state of infancy. Although they are analogous in structure to the idea of weights, topology, neurons the functional units and learning algorithms, they are yet not able to mimic the human brain completely, especially not in tasks that are complex. Their topologies are very simple and their capacity is smaller and the learning algorithms are still very naive. Besides, they cannot be trained to work well for several different tasks at the same time.

As the humans continue to build ANNs to resolve difficult issues such as, for detecting prior unknown kind of malware, we continue to learn more about the human brain and how it accomplishes tasks or some classes of tasks. Make no mistake the ANNs are capable of outperforming human analysts both in terms of speed and accuracy. The action potential in the brain acts within a thousandth of a second while the ANN can classify data of greater magnitude quicker.

For some tasks, the strong points of ANNs augment and support the capabilities of the best human minds with the automation of large workflow. In near future, the ANNs will start to perform added classes of tasks at nearly human levels or possibly super-human levels and thereby becoming structurally and mathematically similar to the biological neural networks.

Can Machine Learning Supersede the Human Brain?

The current boom in the field of artificial intelligence is being powered by the advances in machine learning. They are transforming the industry and how several everyday tasks are done. However what is the future of machine learning? You can see machine learning and artificial intelligence everywhere these days. It is in our phones powering the voice assistants such as Alexa and Siri. It is in the GPS systems providing us the information regarding the fastest route to home. And you can find it on out social media networks proving us targeted advertising and personalized news feeds.

All the artificial intelligence application above rely on machine learning in which case the algorithms are told to act in similar cognition as the human brain. The self-education has already transformed several everyday tasks and continues to do the same in case of many industries. The advantages are clear. Rather than relying on humans to process data and make educated decisions which is very costly and time consuming, the computers can make those judgments seamlessly.

The question is, what happens if the ML goes down the scary path- the one shown in the several sci-fi movies? Is a machine dominated future possible where the machine learning surpasses the human brain? Even if it does not what are the other consequences of the development that we the humans need to consider if we build this technology?

Experts and researchers believe that within 45 years there is 50% chance of artificial intelligence being able to outperform the human brain in all tasks. There are two main kinds of artificial intelligence:

1. Narrow Artificial Intelligence: The artificial intelligence can exhibit some capabilities of the human brain but it lacks in others. As far as the traits that do show the similarity, it has the ability to perform tasks very well. For example, consider AlphaGo AI by DeepMind. It managed to defeat a professional at the game of Go. However, it cannot do much more than that.

2. General Artificial Intelligence: The artificial intelligence possesses all the characteristics associated with the human brain. This includes the capacity to reason, plan, abstract thinking and most importantly learning from experience. This is a big step up from the narrow AI and so it is yet to be completely fulfilled.

The human knowledge resides in the human brain while the machine knowledge resides on the servers. However, the similarities and the differences between a human brain and machine learning go a lot further than that. Although the ANNs (Artificial Neural Networks) can mimic some functions associated with the human brain they have not reached the same level of intelligence. This is mainly because the artificial neurons do not have the capability to self-organize and adapt in the same manner as human neurons can. Apart from that ML cannot be programmed to possess intrinsic human learning characteristics. One of these characteristics is motivation. Humans learn because they love learning new things and find the process to be rewarding. Machines, on the other hand, can only be programmed to work for external rewards or to avoid possible negative consequences. The modern-day computers are capable of memorizing a vast amount of information and undertake supervised complex machine learning tasks. If we look individually these tasks exceed the capabilities of the human brain by far. But as things stand the machines cannot apply knowledge to think in an abstract manner. However, as our dependency on automated tasks grows human learning might evolve in another manner. As most of our answers, these days are just Google away. As a result of this, we can expect the emphasis lessening on information retention in the classrooms of future and get more focused on creativity and issue resolution.

So should we be worried? There has been a lot of hype about the possible negative consequences of ML. However, this thinking neglects to consider the great advantages of a joint ML and human brain learning. Most of the fear of machine learning comes mainly from "singularity" which is a hypothetical point where robots and AI surpass the human brain. The term singularity is derived from a gravitational singularity which happens at the center of the black hole. At this place, the gravitational fields are infinitely powerful and as a result, all laws of physics fail here. Verner Vinge wrote in 1993 applying the term to a time in future when the artificial intelligence will exceed the human intelligence and our lives will be changed forever. This has been the basis for many sci-fi films and stories.

Multiplicity is when humans and machines work together to resolve issues. This doesn't happen in the world of science fiction. This is already a reality in several smart systems in existence today. Humans are a must for multiplicity. A diverse range of people interacts with a range of machines to reciprocate languages, make recommendations on books or even suggest tags for videos and images. This is the approach a lot of people are taking with ML. Machines and humans must evolve together and not apart in silos. Having smarter machines will augment our own capabilities. Similar to a printing press which democratized information and knowledge in the 15th century, the AI and ML are working in today's world.

However, as the ML evolves there are a number of complex and far-reaching queries which need to be answered regarding its applications. For example, how do we know whether the ML is promoting a systemic bias coming out of existing datasets? Another important thing to consider is that humans will lose their purposefulness in a world with no work. We are still coming of age with the artificial intelligence and these things may bear fruit at a time. The next thing to tackle will be the super intelligent AI.

Chapter 5: Twenty Real World Applications of Machine Learning

Managing Large Amount of Data

After such a long period of human existence it is no longer feasible for human beings to monitor and analyze the big and diverse data available in the modern world. The organizations that are data-oriented routinely deal with large volumes of unstructured, semi-structured and structured data. The conventional software and analytics are struggling to keep up as they simply do not have the capacity to analyze the extensive data.

Although a large amount of data has the capacity to help companies streamline operations by using a range of data sets, more and more companies are applying scalable and intelligent solutions to automate their analysis and data processing. This is possible with machine learning. It is a subset of computer science and is a branch of AI (Artificial Intelligence). The ML focusses on study and building of algorithms which learn and make predictions based on available data. It overcomes the limitations of computer programming and makes data-driven decisions.

Machine learning equips the companies to analyze complex data automatically at huge scales with great accuracy. It provides the companies' the insights they require to make data related decisions regarding their operations. Although the ML algorithms need to be educated and trained to enable them with the capacity to deliver the insight. When exposed to large datasets the machines detect patterns and make use of historical and real-time data to determine the best action or procedure to deliver the best results in the shortest period of time.

ML is specifically more useful where there are a large number of data sets having close related or similar values. In some cases, the manual analysis is highly inefficient and impractical and the ML algorithms which are trained to locate specific information can achieve the required efficiency levels in considerably less time.

Machine Learning for Who?

There is a vast range of applications of machine learning. They are limitless from a business perspective. But let's see some examples where industries are typically more focused on data can use ML learning algorithms to provide great insight.

Financial Services

With the growth of financial industry in complexity (because of more stringent regulations to avoid collapse) and scale, the finance companies have been forced to analyze big and varied sets of data to meet the latest regulations related to compliance. As the new regulations require more intricate and comprehensive approach to data analysis the financial companies are looking for more intelligent and automated solutions to increase productivity. They are making use of ML to detect fraudulent activities related to money laundering along with identifying the trade and investment opportunities and assess market risks.

Sales and Marketing

The path leading to a buy is no longer linear as the buyers can engage in businesses via a range of methods from organic search and social media to email marketing. Digital marketing provides you with attribution data; combining it with the options available creates a plethora of client data which needs to be analyzed and action needs to be taken to drive sales and engagement. Due to the valuable and actionable insight gained from the large-scale data without necessary solutions to parsing the data, it becomes difficult to create new strategies. Several businesses are turning to machine learning to interpret diverse data sets by using algorithms to build different correlations. The sales and marketing departments, as a result, are able to synthesize the path leading to the buy and comprehend how they can improve the process.

Data Security

Internet security has quickly moved up the list of agenda of different businesses in recent years. Due to the ransom ware attacks like those by Petya and WannaCry, there has been a renewed emphasis on cyber security. The important thing to remember is that most malware is based on the earlier architecture with just the slight changes made in the code variations. Although these changes are inconspicuous they are difficult to identify for the IT experts right away. And time is of utmost importance while dealing with cyber security threats. However, with ML algorithms the IT experts can breathe a sigh of relief as they can teach the algorithm to analyze malware and look at their variations in the code and in patterns. This enables the algorithms to potentially stop and identify malware attack with accuracy. As the algorithms get richer with more data their capability to protect the digital infrastructure of businesses improves. Ideally, a combination of IT experts and machine learning algorithms is in the best interests of businesses to create a company-wide and strong security.

Real-World Applications of Machine Learning

Machine learning and artificial intelligence are everywhere these days. You are using it in all probability in one way or another and you don't in all probability know about it. The machine learning computers, devices, and software perform through cognition a process similar to that of a human brain. Here are some examples of machine learning which are used every day and you probably are not aware that they are driven by machine learning.

1. Virtual Voice-Activated Personal Assistants

Some of the popular examples of these personal assistants include Alexa, Siri, and Google Now. As its name suggests this software help in finding information when it is requested over voice. All that is needed to be done is activate them and ask them to say" What is the time of my meeting with the boss?" or "When are the flights from New York to Bulawayo?" or such questions. For answering them the personal assistant will look out for suitable information, will recall similar queries placed by you or send commands to other resources such as telephone apps for collecting the information. You may also instruct these assistants for certain tasks such as "Set alarm for 5 AM Monday morning." or "Remind me to go to the visa office tomorrow."

Machine learning has made a significant contribution towards the development of the virtual personal assistants as they gather and process the data and information on the basis of your prior interactions with them. This data is stored and later used to provide results that are tailored to your benefit. They are integrated into different platforms such as:

- Mobile Apps: Google Allo.
- Smart Speakers: Google Home and Amazon Echo.
- Smartphones: Samsung S8 with Samsung Bixby.

2. Predictions During Commuting

Traffic Predictions

The GPS navigation has been in use for some time now. While we are doing that the current location and speeds are getting saved on a central server that manages traffic. The data is used later to create a map of existing traffic. Although this helps in stopping the traffic problems and performs the congestion analysis, the real problem is that only a few cars are equipped with GPS. The ML in such cases helps by estimating the areas where less traffic congestion can be found. They analyze this on the basis of the information collected from their daily experience.

Online Transport Networks

This apps estimate the charges for the ride while booking the cabs. If we are sharing the services how can we minimize the detours? This answer is provided by machine learning. The engineering leader at Uber ATC Jeff Schneider revealed in one interview that they used machine learning to find price surge timings by predicting the demand from the riders. ML plays an important role in the whole cycle of their services.

3. Video Surveillance

Can you imagine a single person monitoring several video cameras at the same time? Well, a difficult task and boring also. Due to this reason the idea of training computers to perform the task made sense. The video surveillance these days is powered by artificial intelligence which makes it possible to detect crime before it is actually committed. They will track unusual pattern of behavior from people standing motionless for long periods or stumbling or taking a nap on benches etc. The ML powered system will alert the human attendants who can avoid the mishaps. When these activities are reported and identified as malicious suitable actions can be taken and the surveillance system, as a result, improves further. This happens because of machine learning presence at the back end.

4. Social Media

Social media platforms are using the machine learning platforms for the user and their own advantage with better-targeted ads and personalizing the news feeds. Here are some examples that you may have noticed, used and loved in the social media accounts. You may not have realized that this is possible only because they are applications using machine learning.

Finding People You Might know

The ML works on a simple concept learning and understanding with experience. The Facebook constantly makes note of the friends you interact with, the personal profiles you visit often, your workplace, your interests or even a group that you frequently share something with. On the basis of constant learning, Facebook will suggest you a list of users you can become friends with.

Face Recognition

If you upload a picture of yourself with a friend the FB recognizes the friend instantly. It will check the projections and poses in the pictures, notice unique attributes and will match them with the people in the list of your friends. The whole process at the back end is complex but takes care of the precision factor and appears like a simple application of machine learning at the front end.

Similar Pins

Machine learning is at the core of computer vision which is the technique used to extract useful information out of videos and images. The computer vision is used by Pinterest to identify pins or objects and it can recommend similar pins as applicable.

5. Malware & Email Spam Filtering

A number of spam filtering methods are used by email clients. These spam filters are constantly updated and they are powered by machine learning. When there is rule-based spam filtering there are chances of it failing to notice the latest wiles adopted by spammers. Decision Tree induction, Multi-Layer Perception are among the many spam filtering techniques to be powered by machine learning.

More than 325,000 malware are detected each day and every code used is similar to the previous version. The ML powered system security programs are capable of understanding the coding pattern. So they detect new malware having 2-10% variation easily and they will protect against them.

6. Online Customer Support

Many sites on the internet these days offer the option of chatting with support representatives while you are navigating on the website. But not every site has live executive available to answer the queries. Most commonly you will talk with a chatbot. The bots tend to collect info from the site and present it to the clients. In the process, the chatbot advances with the experience it has gained with time. They will understand the user queries better and will be able to answer the questions better. This is possible only through machine learning algorithms.

7. Refining Search Engine Results

Search engines such as Google make use of machine learning to improve search results for better observations. Each time you perform a search the algorithm at the back end keeps a watch on how you respond to the offered results. In case you open the top results and stay on the opened pages for long, the search engines will assume that the search results displayed are in accordance with the performed query. Similarly, in case you reach 2nd or 3rd page of search results and not open any of the pages displayed there, the search engine learns that the results displayed there did not match with user requirement. In this manner, the algorithms at the backend of search engines keep improving with search results.

8. Product Recommendations

Once you shop online for some products you start getting emails about suggestions for future shopping. You may notice that the e-commerce website or apps recommend some shopping items that somehow match with your taste? This improves the shopping experience considerably but did you realize how that was possible? It is through machine learning that this magic is possible. On the basis of the pattern generated by your behavior with the app or site along with past purchases, items added to cart, items liked and brand recommendations etc., product recommendations are created.

9. Online Fraudulent Transactions Detection

The ML is certainly fulfilling its potential in terms of making the cyberspace a secure place for transactions. It can track the monetary fraudulent transactions online and that in itself is a primary thing in its favor. For example, PayPal uses machine learning for protection against laundering online. The online company uses a set of tools for comparing millions of transactions taking place and distinguish between legitimate and illegal transactions taking place online between buyers and sellers.

10. Walking Talking (Humanoid) Robots Using Imitation Learning

Imitation learning is related to observational learning which a behavior pattern is displayed by toddlers and infants. It also happens to be the umbrella category for reinforcement learning. It is a challenge of getting an agent out there in the real world to maximize the rewards. Probabilistic or Bayesian models are common features of the machine approach. The thought of using imitation learning for humanoid robots was floated way back in 1999. Nowadays the imitation learning has become an integral part in the field of robotics. Characteristics such as mobility in the factories such as agriculture, construction and military make it extremely useful for robotic solutions. Humanoid robots are developing grasping techniques by using imitation learning which as you can imagine will be useful everywhere.

11. Bioinformatics

Machine learning has a number of new and emerging applications in the field of bioinformatics. Bioinformatics is a mathematical and computational approach to processing and understanding biological data. The ML techniques like deep learning empower the algorithms to use the automatic feature learning that means based on dataset patterns alone the algorithms can combine a number of features of input data to create an abstract set of features for further learning. Machine learning is used in six fields of bioinformatics viz, proteomics, system biology, text mining, evolution, microarrays, and genomics.

12. Text and Hypertext Categorization

Automatic categorization of text is an important area even for research. In the last two decades the advancement of hypertext documents such as web pages has made development in the field a necessity. The text and hypertext classifiers developed by the machine learning algorithms have been found to be much cheaper and quicker to build than those developed by the knowledge engineering. They are more accurate as well in case of some applications.

13. Stock Market Trading

The classification algorithms of machine learning can be utilized for predicting the stock market variations. There are some supervised learning classification models available in the market. A set of data is provided to the ML classification algorithm with each belonging to a different category. The categories could be buying or selling stocks. This classification algorithm develops a model based on the data set available and then classifies the data into one of the categories.

14. Automatic Translation

Everyone knows about Google Translate which is a site capable of translating between 100 human languages like it is magic. It is available on smartwatches and smartphones. The machine learning technology behind Google Translate is termed as Machine Translation. It has allowed people to communicate with quarters where communication was not possible in the past. In the last couple of years, deep learning has completely rewritten the approach to machine translation. The technology is called sequence-to-sequence learning.

15. Self-Driving Cars

Nowadays the machine learning algorithms are used extensively for finding out solutions to different challenges coming up in self-driving cars. By incorporating the ECU (Electronic Sensor Data) inside a car, the machine learning has been enabled for accomplishing new tasks. Apart from the car driving by itself, the other potential applications include evaluation of driving conditions by using data from a range of sensors such as radars, lidar, IoT or cameras. In an autonomous car, one of the major tasks for the ML algorithms is a constant rendering of information about the surrounding environment and forecasting the changes in it to the driver.

16. Smart Computers

A smart computer is a device which is embedded with M2M (machine to machine) and cognitive learning technologies such as machine learning, artificial intelligence, and deep learning. It uses technology to solve problems, reason, make decisions and in the end take action. Understanding human language was one of the most difficult tasks for a computer beyond basic verbs the bots had generally failed at figuring out the variance in the written words. But they are very good at information retrieval. Google's search algorithm can shake down 90 billion web pages in a whisker. So they are likely to become smarter than humans in certain areas eventually.

17. Spotify

Spotify knows you better than you yourself. On every Monday they provide their millions of users a fresh new playlist called Discover Weekly. It is a mix of 30 songs they have never heard before but will in all probability love. It is possible because of machine learning. Algorithms have become capable of analyzing audio content as they can perform music identification, playlist creation, analysis, and personalized recommendations. Spotify used three kinds of recommendation models. None of them is a revolutionary model rather they mix some of the better strategies used by other services for creating their own powerful and unique discovery engine. For creating Discover Weekly they use these recommendation models:

- Collaborative filtering model which analyzes your and others behavior.
- NLP (Natural Language Processing) models that analyze text.
- An audio model which analyses raw audio tracks by themselves.

18. Shadow Profiles

This is how Facebook figures out about everyone you have ever met. Shadow profiles or contact information has been a known feature of Facebook for a few years. But most users are not aware of its power and reach. The shadow profile connections happen inside the Facebook black box and they are powered by machine learning. You will not realize how comprehensive the data mining of your lives has become until an uncanny recommendation comes up. Facebook uses the algorithm called People You May Know and its results are pretty obvious.

19. Biometrics

In the field of behavioral biometrics deep learning, artificial intelligence and machine learning are all in together. The biometrics identify people by how they interact with online applications and devices. Biometrics is a dynamic modality and unlike something that someone possesses such as a token or a device, it is totally passive and works from the background. That makes it impossible to steal or copy. The biometrics has developed so much that it can capture as many as 2000 attributes just from a mobile device use. These include the way the person is holding the phone, scrolls, exchanging between different fields, the pressure used while typing and how they respond to various stimuli appearing in the online applications. It is used primarily for stopping the use of stolen identities while applying for online credit and preventing the takeovers of accounts once the person is logged into a session. Remember most fraudulent transactions occur within authenticated sessions.

20. Self-Replicating Machines

Engineers and scientists have toyed with the idea of building self-replicating machines since 1940s. They were called Von Newmann machines as they being named after John Von Newmann. With the recent advancements in the field of 3D printing such as zero gravity and machine learning, the self-replicating machines have become a possible reality of today. Google has a system called AutoML which recently created a series of ML codes having greater rate of efficiency than those who created the codes. In this latest blow to human supremacy the robot students have become self-replicating masters. AutoML was created because there wasn't enough top quality talent available in the field of machine learning. There just aren't enough engineers with cutting edge available to keep up with the demand. AutoML is a genesis for new generation of ML. The machines of tomorrow will not just learn but they will self-update and will be capable of programming themselves to solve unforeseen issues.

Chapter 6: What is Predictive Analytics?

For several companies, huge data - really big volumes of unstructured, semi-structured and raw structured data is an untapped source of information that can aid business decisions and improve operations. As this data continues to change and diversify, more and more companies are taking to predictive analytics to tap the source and make benefits from the large-scale data.

There is a common miscomprehension that machine learning and predictive analytics are one and the same. That is not the case. They do overlap in one area however and that is predictive modeling. Basically, predictive analytics includes a range of statistical techniques including ML, data mining and predictive modeling and uses historical and current statistics for estimating or predicting future outcome. This outcome could be the behavior of a customer during the purchase or probable changes in the market. It helps us to guess the possible future occurrences with the analysis of past pattern.

How Does Predictive Analytics Work?

The predictive analytics gets driven by predictive modeling. It is an approach rather than a process. ML and predictive analytics are hand-in-hand because the predictive models typically include ML algorithms. The created models can be trained over a period of time to react to new values or other data thereby delivering the results needed by the organization.

There are two kinds of predictive models. One is the classification model which predicts class membership and the second is the regression model that predicts numbers. The models are made from algorithms which perform data mining and statistical analysis to determine patterns and trends in the data. The predictive analytics software will have built-in algorithms which can be used to create predictive models. Algorithms are called as classifiers and they identify the set of categories to which the data belongs.

Commonly Used Predictive Models

The most widely used predictive models are:
- Regression (Linear and logistic)
- Decision Trees
- Neural Networks

Regression (Linear and logistic)
It is one of the more popular methods available in statistics. Regression analysis provides a relationship between variables and finds key patterns in diverse and big data sets. It also finds out how they relate to each other.

Decision Trees
The decision trees are simple yet powerful forms of multiple variable analysis. Decision trees are produced by algorithms which identify different ways of splitting the data into branch-like segments. They partition the data into subsets depending on various categories of input variables. It helps you understand a user's path to a decision.

Neural Networks
They are built on the patterns of the neurons in the human brain. Neural networks are often referred to as artificial neural networks and are a variance of deep learning technology.

They are commonly used to solve difficult pattern recognition situations and are unbelievably useful for analyzing big data sets. They are very good at handling nonlinear data relationships and also work well when some variables are unknown.

Classifiers

Every classifier approaches the data in a different manner so, for the managers to get the results they require they must select right classifiers and models.

- Clustering algorithms: They organize data into different groups with similar members.
- Time Series algorithms: They plot the data sequentially and are useful in forecasting constant values over a period of time.
- Outlier Detection algorithms: They focus completely on anomaly detection, identifying events, observations or items that don't conform to a specific expected pattern or standards in a data set.
- Ensemble Models: These models make use of several ML algorithms for obtaining a better predictive performance than compared to the output expected from a single algorithm.
- Naive Bayes: This classifier permits you to predict a category or a class based on a provided set of features by using probability.
- Factor Analysis: It is a method used for describing variations and aims at finding independent latency in variables.
- Support Vector Machines: They are a supervised kind of machine learning technique that uses associated learning algorithms for analyzing data and recognizing patterns.

Machine Learning and Predictive Analytics Applications

The companies that are overflowing with data are struggling to turn all the information into useful insight. For these organizations, ML and predictive analytics can arrange the solution. No matter how big the data is if it cannot be used to enhance the external and internal processes and meet objectives it becomes a useless resource. Predictive analysis is used more commonly in marketing, security, risks, fraud detection and operations. Here are some of the examples of how machine learning and predictive analytics are used in various industries:

Financial Services and Banking: In the financial services and banking industry, ML and predictive analytics are used together to measure market risks, detect and decrease fraud, identify opportunities and there are several other uses.

Security: Cyber security is at the top of the agenda for almost all businesses in the modern world. It is no surprise that ML and predictive analytics play a key role in security aspects. The security organizations use predictive analysis often to improve their performance and services. They can detect anomalies, understand client behavior, detect fraud and as a result, they enhance data security.

Retail: The retail industry is using ML for understanding customer behavior better. Who is buying what and where? They want to know the answer to these queries. These questions can be answered with accurate predictive models and data sets thereby helping retailers to plan beforehand and stock items based on consumer trends and seasonality. Improves the ROI a great deal.

Developing The Right Environment

Although predictive analytics and ML can be a huge boost for most companies, implementing these solutions halfheartedly without consideration for their fitment into everyday operations will only hinder their potency to deliver the insight the company needs. To get the best out of ML and predictive analytics, companies need to make sure that they have the architecture to support the solutions along with high-quality data which will help them in learning. Data preparation and its quality are the key portions of predictive analytics.

The input data which may span across several platforms and consist of multiple data sources need to be centralized and unified in a coherent way. For achieving this the companies need to develop good reliable data governance programs to govern the overall data management and make sure that only the high-quality data gets captured and used. Another thing is, the current processes might have to be altered to include ML and predictive analytics as this will enable companies to have efficiency at all points of the business. And most importantly the companies must know what issues they want to be resolved as it will aid them in determining the most suitable model for use.

Predictive Models

The IT experts and data scientists working in an organization are normally tasked with selecting or developing the right predictive models or possibly build one for themselves to satisfy the organization needs. However, these days the ML and predictive analytics is not just the area of expertise for mathematicians, data scientists, and statisticians but there are business consultants and analyst working in the area. More and more people in businesses are using the models to develop insights and improve operations. However, there are issues when they employ are not aware of what model to use or how to deploy it or in the case when they need some information immediately. There is sophisticated software available to help the employees with the problem.

Chapter 7: What is Data Mining?

Data mining means extracting knowledge out of huge quantities of data. In other words, we can say that it is a process of discovering different kinds of patterns inherited in the data sets which are new, useful and accurate. Data mining is an iterative process which creates descriptive and predictive models by uncovering previously unknown patterns and trends in a large quantity of data. This exercise is executed to support decision making. It is basically a subset of business analytics and is similar to experimental research. Origins of data mining can be found in statistics and databases. ML, on the other hand, works with algorithms that improve automatically via experience they gain out of data. In other words, in machine learning, we discover new algorithms from experience. These algorithms of ML can extract information automatically but the source used for machine learning is also data. It involves two kinds of data, one is test data and the second is the training data. Data mining techniques are commonly used in machine learning and along with the learning algorithms it is used to build models of what is happening behind the scenes to predict the outcome of the future.

What is data mining and what is the relationship between ML and data mining? Data Mining means extracting knowledge out of a big amount of data. It was introduced in 1930 and at first it was referred to as knowledge discovery in database. Data mining is utilized to get rules out of existing data. Its origins lie in conventional databases having unstructured data. It is implemented where you can develop your own models and the data mining techniques are used. It is more natural and involves more involvement of human beings. They are used in cluster analysis. Data mining is abstracted from data warehousing. It is more of a research using methods similar to ML but is applied in limited sectors.

Data Mining Techniques

The specialists working in the field of data mining rely on techniques and intersection of statistics, database management, and machine learning. They have dedicated their careers to understanding what conclusions are to be drawn from a huge amount of information. What are the techniques used for turning this into reality? Data mining is effective when it draws on some of these techniques for their analysis:

1. Tracking Pattern

One of the fundamental techniques used in data mining is learning to recognize patterns in the data sets. Normally this is an aberration in the data which is happening at some intervals or a flaw or an ebb in some variables over a period of time. For example, you may observe that sale of certain product spike up immediately before holidays. Or you may notice that warm weather drives people to your site.

2. Classification

It is a more complex data mining technique that asks you to collect different attributes together in discernable categories which can be later used to arrive at further conclusions or serve in some other function. For example, in case you are evaluating the data on independent client's financial background and purchase history you may be able to classify the individuals as high, medium or low-risk candidates for credit. You can then use the classifications to learn more about the clients.

3. Association

This is related more to tracking patterns however, it is more specifically involved in the dependently linked variables. In the case of an association, you look for specific attributes or events which are correlated to other attributes or events. For example, you may notice that when your customer purchases some specific item they also buy another related item.

This sequence of events is used to populate the "people also bought" section in the online store.

4. Outlier Detection

In some cases just identifying the overreaching pattern cannot give you a clear understanding of the data set. You are also required to understand the anomalies also called outliers in the data. For example, your buyers are almost exclusively male, however, during a single week in July there is a sudden rise in female buyers. You may want to investigate the reason for the event and find out what drove the sales so, you can either replicate it or understand the behavior of your audience better.

5. Clustering

This is similar to classification, however, involves grouping of chunks of data together which is similar. For example, you may select to cluster different demographics of the customers in various packets based on how much extra income they earn or how often they are shopping at the online store.

6. Regression

Regression is used basically as a form of modeling and planning. It is used to find out the chances of presence of certain variables because some other variables are there. For example, you may use this to project some price based on factors such as consumer demand, competition, and availability. More specifically the main focus of regression is in helping you uncover exact relationships between two or more variables inside a specific data set.

7. Prediction

It is easily one of the most valuable data mining techniques used. This is because it is used for predicting the kind of data you will see in future. In some cases, just by understanding and recognizing the historical trends we can chart an accurate prediction of what will happen in the future. For example, we can see the credit history of clients and their past buys to predict whether there will be a credit risk in future in case a loan is extended.

Chapter 8: How to Optimize your Business

Optimizing your business involves a process of measuring productivity, efficiency, and performance of your business and finding out methods for improving the measures. It is an act of taking the older business process and optimizing it for quality. However, the means for achieving it differ quite a lot. The business process optimization happens to be one of the last steps used in BPM (Business Process Management). It is a method that advocates a continuous process re-evaluation and improvement. Therefore in order to make it work, you must carry out the first three steps necessary for any BPM initiative. These steps are:

1. Process Identification

You must already be aware of the process which you need to optimize. In a lot of cases, you will select processes that are critical for the organization and are drivers for the profits. After all, what is the point of performing the optimization if it cannot have any impact?

2. Business Process Mapping

Until you have mapped the business process you will have a difficult time finding out possible improvements. In case you don't map for the business process you can do it with a flowchart by using just a pen and paper or by using workflow software.

3. Business Process Analysis

Before beginning the improvement activity in a business process you need to analyze every step first. This analysis can either be completely straightforward with some totally obvious possible changes or could be a lot more difficult in case the issues are not so apparent. In case of later, you can make use of some of the tools used for business process improvement to find out the minute inefficiencies.

After completing this, with all that out of the way you need to have a clearly mapped out and defined process and a few ideas about how to optimize the same.

Step 1: Identifying What Needs To Be Optimized

There are many methods that can be used for optimizing your business processes. This depends on the process that is selected for optimization. You cannot find one size that will fit the description for all. However, in most cases, the optimization is performed by either process improvement or automation.

Re-structuring, or Process Improvement is quite simple and it just takes a good look at every step in the process. The idea in this method is to find out the processes that are:

Wasteful: Every step in a process must add some value to the end target which could be some output or certain value. And the process must collect to something in the context of company goals. Many times you will find that some steps or processes are useless without the creation of some value. There are different kinds of wastes and wasteful processes.

Inefficient and Improvable: This means that a process or a step is just not as efficient as it may be. For example, there may be a lot more steps being taken than required. One of the most glaring examples of this is the approval processes. In case you are trying to have a new project off the ground, you are required to get approvals from senior management in the company. Meaning you will be required to wait for more than five very busy executives to find time to read documents and provide green light.

Once you have found out the steps or processes that fall in these categories you will be required to improve them for quality. This can be achieved by restructuring the process meaning by changing the steps or restructuring the steps by eliminating the useless steps or processes or by doing a bit of both.

Step 2: Consider Automation

Many people don't like manual work. Many times it makes you feel as if you are a cog in the machine doing things that robots can do better. All you need to do is find the right tools or software for the work. The BPA (Business Process Automation) can help you with taking out manual labor from your employees' workload and this leads to better productivity and morale as the employees will work on what matters. No one likes the grunt work. Automation varies with tasks. Here are some examples of automation:

Customer Support

In case you are working with your business associates online you will have customer support form open on the site. Let's say there is an issue with the new software update and as a result, 10% of the user base is getting affected. This means your inbox is getting really clogged with emails about complaints. Although the first bug report is very useful the rest is only a clutter and you have to reply to it all. There is software available which allows you to create events in which case you can send automatic replies to the complaints depending on keywords mentioned in the ticket.

Social Media Management

Whatever the organization is about, the employees will have Facebook accounts in all probability or at least LinkedIn pages. The conventional ways of managing the pages are to have someone log in manually and then find something to post 3-4 times every day. Instead of wasting your time doing all this you can use a social media tool to plan your posts right through the next month.

There are other examples which might be more relevant to your business. But many such solutions are available online to help you out in your business process automation endeavor.

Step 3: Adopting Technology and Total Process Change

Adopting the correct technology will always be the game changer. Unlike the first two approaches, this doesn't exactly optimize the process as such. Instead, it changes it totally. Let's say that you make use of the whiteboard to organize your daily chores with the organization. By adopting the task management software you can improve the daily efficiency of businesses without actually changing any process. By having software in charge you will see benefits such as:

- **Less Mistakes and Missed Deadlines:** Humans are notorious for making errors. Everyone can mess up once in a while or forget something important or miss a deadline. The task management software ensures that this doesn't happen as it reminds you of the daily tasks and ensuing deadlines.
- **Central Command Center:** It is much easier to create new tasks online and pin them to your employees instead of sending them detailed emails and hope that it doesn't get overlooked or lost. For more process-oriented examples there is workflow management software available. Rather than having to keep track of workflow manually via chat or email you can use dedicated systems to manage all the processes via a single dashboard. This automatically eliminates many issues you will encounter with process management like,
- **Lack of Standardization in Processes:** It is very difficult to make all your employees follow different procedures at the same time. The workflow software ensures that everyone is completing all the required steps in the process in the correct order.

- **Simpler Tracking and Analysis:** The workflow software allows easier tracking than compared to the average process maps. Without the software, you will need to keep track of the processes manually through email and chat. Additionally the software measures process efficiency as otherwise, you will have to manually gather all the data from different reports, employees and software.

Therefore for optimizing the business processes, you need to identify the weak and inefficient processes, map them out and analyze them. Find out if there are any better ways of doing them. Then optimize them by either restructuring them, automating or adopting some technology that will totally change the way things worked.

Step 4: Optimizing the Business Resources

When you are hiring for startups there is a golden rule, recruit only when the existing employees are 120% stretched. Simply put the startups cannot take employees who cannot be 100% utilized. There isn't any room for excess baggage. Although this makes sense in business terms you can also bring down the moral of the employees by overworking them. The answer is in optimizing the business resources so that it is possible to extract better productivity from the team before starting the recruitment of new people.

Value Over Volume

One of the fastest and yet more difficult decisions to take for the startup owners is optimization of business resources. It is a difficult decision to have value over volume. It probably means raising the value of the product or services in a way that the volume of transactions comes down but due to the higher margins, the revenue actually goes up. Employees now will have more time to finish their tasks and as a result, can provide a better quality of service to existing clients. All this is easier said than done though and the decisions need to be taken after careful deliberations.

Reduce Waste

Waste is a big problem, especially in consumable businesses. Not only does it increase the operational cost but can also overwork and frustrate the employees by forcing them to produce items that might get thrown away eventually. Better prediction models and forecasting tools will aid in optimizing the operations, reducing the workload of employees and increase revenues in the process.

Re-engineering the Operations

It is a common practice for startup employees to don many hats at work to take care of different tasks at the same time. Studies have indicated that splitting the attention across several tasks can decrease the productivity and increase the time required to complete every task by as much as 25%. Although having to play multiple roles is a part of the startup business there may still be able to re-engineer operations so that these employees can focus on one thing at a time. For example, in case you have a marketer who looks after all the digital activities you can rearrange their workload by making them focus on email marketing just on a single day of the week.

Outsourcing the Non-Value Adding Work

There is no need to do all the work in-house. Many consulting firms have devoted staffs that are capable of taking care of different tasks such as preparing presentations or aggregating the spreadsheets. Although these tasks are significant, it does not make sense for consultants having high values rates to perform them. Startups can take inspiration from the outsourcing to perform similarly and outsource some tasks to some data processing industry that can take care of all non-value-adding task items and release the company employees from tedious work. These tasks could be trivial such as submitting taxi receipts for compensation or something more significant such as converting a Word document into PPT for presentation. From the business point of view, it may increase the costs but it also increases the efficiency of your team dramatically. In turn, it helps in accelerating business growth.

Using Third-Party Tools

When you are a new business, it is important to focus all resources on the core specialties. It means avoiding working on things that do not directly contribute toward making the product or service better. For example, you may integrate your software with the third party tools which help in achieving some functionalities without the organization having to build the features yourself. Uber is one of the more popular startups in the world and its app still runs on Google Maps. By not working on the mapping portion of their requirement themselves Uber was able to arrive in the market sooner and that has contributed a great deal to their success.

Business optimization rationale in new businesses is pretty simple: The bootstrapped businesses cannot afford inefficiency. The basic rule is to look into every task performed by employees in your company objectively and ask yourself these questions, can this task be scrapped altogether? Can it be outsourced? Can the process be optimized to improve efficiency?

Step 5: Optimizing Business Operations

Business operations can always be improved for any organization. In fact, honing efficiency and effectiveness is critical for a middle market corporation. You will need all the available resources to encompass the next stage of growth and be capable of managing competition from larger organizations. Instead of working at a smaller scale and keeping on fixing sporadic problems, one is better off at using one of these strategies to address various aspects of the operations. Here are some strategies that will help in shaking loose the operations section and free resources which can be utilized better in some other areas.

Take the "Lean" Approach

An operational philosophy, "LEAN" focuses on improving operational activities continuously so that you deliver products and services to your clients with higher internal and external value. By having practices that cause value addition and avoiding the practices that do not, the company makes its operations department more efficient. There are organizations that have a worksheet to aid executives to determine whether their companies are actually employing lean practices or are only working on some related jargon.

Focusing on Quality

There are several versions of quality management available in business theories for many years like "statistical process control" by W Edwards Deming, the total quality movement of the 1980s or other practices such as six sigma. These practices were originally intended for production but later expanded in operational work of the organizations. The main idea is to reduce work and wastage thereby saving money in the process, improving results and making the organization more effective.

Improving Forecasting

Whether you are selling products or services, buying and managing inventory, controlling supply chains or correctly staffing the company, all organizations try to forecast the demand. Several companies are not very good at forecasting but it only means that they are not prepared to meet the market demands or are wasting money and activities on keeping over capacity. According to the NCMM whitepaper, the bourbon distiller Maker's Mark broadcasted that it will have to water its products because of low-quality forecasting.

As they were not able to satisfy their clients they were irate. Luckily for the middle market companies, sophisticated tools are available with extensive knowledge to improve forecasting of all kinds.

Introducing Customer Focused Thinking

The management teams are always fond of saying how customer-centric their organizations are. Match it with your experience as a customer and now think how many organizations place their customers first. The customer-centric approach by any business is unbelievably efficient. In the end, it is the customers and their perception and attitude towards a business that decides its fate. You need to focus your strategy and operations to embrace the customers and keep them satisfied and happy. If you can do that you are on a fast path to success in business.

Business Process Re-engineering (The Good Old BPR)

BPR (Business Process Reengineering) at one point of time was a craze among company management. Organizations were trying to rework their operational process to achieve greater efficiency. Much similar to all fads it was a lot of talks and very little action. The idea, however, has not lost its credibility as business processes develop over a period of time. As the conditions change, organizations keep adopting and adding to the processes. In the end, you will have a difficult process going that was designed by a committee. However, with real re-engineering, organizations can isolate the wasteful processes in the running of the business and develop better and more effective processes. During re-engineering, the business processes remember to have the frontline employees involved. They are the ones who actually know how things take place and they might even have inputs on how to make things better.

Step 6: Performing Research to Predict Product Trends

Predicting the product trends is like catching the wave nobody has seen coming. It requires deep understanding of the niche market and it can guide your investments in future in right and profitable direction. There are some processes you can adopt for the purpose to be able to predict the product trends.

Predicting, remember is a risky business and can prove to be costly if done incorrectly. Let's learn how to identify trends and differentiate them from the temporary craze so that your company's future is safe.

Performing the right research is essential in predicting the future of your products. There are several methods for researching product trends. Let's see some of them:

Trade Journals

In order to learn about your industry be sure to read some of the trade journals. For example, in case you are selling from the Home and Kitchen section you can take a look at "Home Accents Today". In this manner you see what the experts in the industry are discussing. As you are going through the journal look for patterns for specific products. Contemplate which of the products will emerge as the winner from the patterns.

Social Media

Always keep an eye on the trends that appear on the social media pages. You will find some people behaving and communicating in certain manner as well as make up their minds on some buying options. One example is people posting opinions, content or web links all across the FB walls. Some special social groups are created on different platforms that are active followers of the specific product or industry.

Participate on Forums and Discussion Boards

You can find forums on pretty much any niche in the world. Find one where the customers are discussing their opinions about various products from an industry. At times they can even provide ideas which will inspire some innovation.

Read Articles

Find out articles that are specific to your industry. You might find some hidden gems there that will give you an insight into the industry future.

Advertisements

Trends do not exist in isolation. Advertisements can lead to clues as to what lies ahead. Look for patterns in them and watch out for the marketing terms such as eco-friendly or vegan. The advertisers are in line with what is trendy with the consumers.

Product Tracking Software

You will also need to perform some current product sales research before you start predicting the product trends more accurately. For example you can easily find how ASIN is doing by inputting ASIN in the "Trendster". Use the statistics you find along with the insight to develop your understanding of market behavior.

When you have gone through all these resources you would have gathered the information necessary for going to the next step.

Step 7: Observing Patterns and Prediction. Differentiate between real trends and momentary crazes

Observing patterns is where the context plays its part. There is a large picture and small picture in the product trends and there are several trends which give birth to new product trends. As you go through the freshly gathered information you will start to see patterns. When you perform some careful analysis and pay attention to the overlapping of trending categories you will see the potential for the products. For example, in case you are researching trends for fitness training, outdoor living and advanced technology, although these trends may not appear to be connected they lead to products such as a smart watch with a heart rate monitor. You may consider market demand and context to develop new products which are innovative and they might become trends on their own. It will be a grave error to underestimate the power of context and it might be a great to have it right.

It is important to remember that you are trying to predict product trends and not the momentary fads that hit the market. As the trend can go on for years or even decades while the craze is likely to live for a season at the most. It fades and it is fairly easy to spot the craze in case you consider some factors. The real thing must have these:

- Inherent Utility: Does the specific item serve any useful purpose? Or is it relying on specific circumstances to show its usefulness?
- Long-term value: Will people still love the product in a few years? Will it survive the change of season?
- Does it mold with other trends? - Does it make sense to use it in a broader context of the industry? As was mentioned before, the trends do not exist in isolation. One example is Acai which exploded in popularity in the last decade due to the quality it has as an organic super fruit. But it also tastes good. So the Acai trend fits with other trends such as novelty, health and awareness.

Being able to predict the product trends is being a step ahead of the competition. It provides you a priceless opportunity to go to the market with something completely new. Following the steps provides great insight which refines your understanding of the market and its variance. When you have discovered a trend study it to ensure that it is not just a craze and perform the research. Many sellers make the mistake of assuming that just because a product is popular it will continue to sell highly. But to be certain that you have found a trend, you may want to see other products in the category and how they are doing right now. A quick search online can reveal crucial information about the sales of a specific product. It helps you arrive to accurate conclusions about the trends.

Step 8: Building a Data-Driven Strategy

In order to ensure that the marketing section is contributing effectively towards the business, you need a customizable data-driven strategy. Data reveals the strengths and weaknesses of all parts of your business thereby allowing you to take strategic decisions to develop a marketing strategy for success. Most marketers feel that data is any company's most underused asset. So how to incorporate data-driven marketing in your business and start enjoying the benefits? Here are some steps you can follow to make sure that you are using data to effectively run the marketing strategy:

1. Determining your goals

There is one important step before you start data collection and that is knowing which data is worth collecting. Decide what kind of data will have a positive impact on the marketing strategy. Leave out the data that will not be used to add the effectiveness of the strategy and focus on collecting data around key KPIs which can actually move the things along.

2. Building your team

Before beginning to analyze data it is significant to build a team to handle it. The team must include members from various departments and cross-disciplinary sections. Richard Baystom suggested on Effin Amazing that it doesn't mean that someone from IT gets together with someone from sales just collecting the guys the managers can spare. It means that you find people who are willing to go beyond their area of expertise and knowledge. For example, you need data scientists who are willing to learn about marketing or IT people who are willing to learn about sales. Prioritizing the collaboration of these people by scheduling focused frequent meeting is critical. In the meetings, everyone shares their ideas and information and can take the credit when the team is successful.

3. Gathering the Data

When you are ready to start gathering the data you need to ensure that you place it in one place for easy analysis. Think about collecting the following kind of data:
- Competitors.
- Targeted market.
- Marketing.
- Social media analytics (impressions, click-throughs, conversions etc.).
- Customer data including personal, transaction data, online activity, and social network activity.
- Qualitative and Prospect data.

There are even more kinds of data. You can begin by asking the different members of the team what kind of data they prepare and use and gather all kind of information you can from other departments also. Jim Bergeson has pointed out in an article that data is sometimes hidden in the innermost resources of your company maybe with the vendors or dealers or resellers of the product or services. It could be with the sales people or even locked up in an IT section vault.

Once this data exploration is done you will learn what is happening at all stages of the customer lifecycle with information such as, problems at the sales point, complaints or service calls, referrals, subsequent purchases, and online recommendations.

4. Evaluating the data & Taking Action

Evaluate the collected data against the KPIs and start using this data to drive the marketing strategies.

- *Refine the content marketing strategy:* You may already be using the content marketing strategy to attract and engage the audience. But sometimes there is no clear strategy behind the content or you do not have a clear idea about who you are trying to reach. However, once you have the data to make educated decisions you are on your way. You can maybe combine the sales and marketing strategies together to make more money. You can also experiment with different kinds of content such as GIFs, images and videos. In case you are already putting out good content regularly this step should not be a problem. However, do not forget the most important part and that is engagement. When you provide your customers what they want they are more likely to be engaged in the content. It will need some trial and error but the data will aid you in determining the best way to engage the audience.
- *Consider new Submarkets:* Once you have all the insight from the collected data you can begin creating new submarkets for your products and services. This doesn't mean that you need to change the brand entirely, perhaps you just need to modify who you are selling your product to. For example, in case you are currently selling custom signage for the birthday parties and you find out that there is a massive demand for similar products for weddings, you may wish to tweak the marketing strategy a little to target engaged couples and perhaps create a new line

for them. The overall target is to look for opportunities in the niche and serve the new audience with your products and services.

- *Removing the Hurdles*: The collected data will also reveal the possible hurdles potential clients are facing in the sales process. This is the time to address these issues. Are your customers getting stuck with the product items in the cart? How can you make them complete the purchase? One of the examples is Pura Vida bracelets. The company promotes the products via content on Facebook and they recently offered a time-sensitive discount for the fan page to motivate the shoppers.

- *Exploring alternative marketing channels:* Sometimes you discover that your business is not reaching all the necessary customers. In case your site is the only channel you are using to share information about your products and services your business will not sustain. The collected data can help you look into other channels and ways. You might want to try the co-marketing opportunities with other businesses having different products than your own or start an affiliate program in which the high-value customers spread a word about your products in exchange of discounts or some other benefits. By analyzing the collected data you will start to understand what channels are most suitable for your products and services.

- *Do not stop testing*: Although data can aid in the development of new marketing strategies, it needs to be frequently tested and managed. In "New Breed Marketing" Matthew Buckley states that you need to test your marketing efforts with small experiments which can be achieved in a single day. He suggested the use of scientific methods to do so. The target is to gather all the important data quickly and proficiently so that you can carry on drawing conclusions from it and even build new experiments. More the testing you perform on the data more informed is your marketing efforts.

Achieving the truly data-driven marketing effort is challenging. A study from CMO Council and RedPointGlobal which is titled "Empowering the Data-Driven Customer Strategy: Addressing Customer Engagement from the Foundation Up" points to four hurdles which will keep the marketers from moving the developed strategies towards execution. The issues include a lack of real-time data, lack of internal cohesiveness, and lack of technology and customer focus. The study describes that only 7% of the marketers are saying that they can always deliver data-driven, real-time experiences across several physical and digital touch points. Although 52% marketers asserted that they can deliver most of the experiences, they could do so only via digital channels or marketing owned channels. So, in reality, many companies are having trouble in gathering and analyzing data across various channels in real time.

In order to achieve a real triumph in data-driven marketing, businesses need the right kind of technology. One-third of people say that they invested in five out of ten independent platforms or solutions in the last five years however many still don't have the requisite tools to visualize their data fully. The real issue is the connectivity between the solutions. About 3% of marketers are saying that all their systems are totally in sync thereby connecting all the data, metrics and the insight smoothly across all channels. 15% admitted that they have no strategy at all for the development of internal processes and technologies in order to adopt newer cloud solutions in their legacy infrastructure.

Step 9: Targeting and Connecting with Potential Customers

In case you are rolling out new marketing plans or are looking to provide a facelift to the current one, here are some ways to help you connect with the customers and foster some leads. Arriving at a right and effective marketing strategy is not an easy task. You need to make decisions about who you think the clients are then spending a huge amount of time collecting and analyzing data about their buying habits. It is both expensive and time-consuming. But this monetary and time-consuming investment may yield results that are game-changing for the organization. If you are beginning to formulate a marketing strategy and netting some customers here are the steps to take for success

1. Identify the Customers

You will not be able to connect positively with your potential clientele in case you do not have the potential clients in mind. Survey the current customers along with members of the targeted market. This is to find out how you may improve your presentation of your products and services or what is missing from what is being offered by you at the moment. Throw a large net to capture people that are interested in your products and services and use their data to develop your brand in a better way to resonate with the targeted market. When you know about the audience, where they hang out on the internet and what they react to, then you can start marketing.

2. Research the competitors to find out their customers

A simple way to find out the most effective marketing campaign for your products is by researching your competitors. Not only the simple exercise will provide an insight into the ideas for your own campaigns it will reveal the dark areas in the competitor's modus operandi and provide new directions for you. If you are going in a business from the same industry you will eventually compete with the competitor for the same targeted market. So might as well use their example to improve your products and services.

3. Targeted Advertisements

For an economical and yet effective method of advertising, Google and Facebook prove that just a little bit can go a long way. Although most of the advertising in the real world reaches those who come across the billboards, commercials or bus stops, these targeted ads are capable of locating people that are most likely to need your services based on their geographical locations, demographics (such as age, education, gender and status of relationship), browsing activities and interests. With investment in the targeted ads and paying via their PPC (Pay Per Click) or PPI (Pay Per Impression) methods, the organizations can see significant bumps in user engagements, sales, and most importantly conversion.

4. Social Media Use

There is a huge difference in having a little bit of presence on social media and having the social media presence. When you are trying to keep your customers, a bit more effort on Twitter, Facebook and Instagram go a long way. Many businesses just use their accounts to only promote their company. But smart social media operators strategize the relevant posts, links to great articles and answer customer queries as soon as they are asked. As a result, they are giving customers the impression that they are human beings who genuinely care. These are the organizations that retain their customers. Provide the users with new ways of using their products or services and help to solve issues as and when they arise.

5. Respond to all Communication

When a guy called Paul English was leading Kayak he used one of the most valuable practices ever. He insisted that there was an extremely annoying and loud phone right in the middle of his office. This was for receiving customer complaints. This practically ensured that the calls were answered by everyone including developers, engineers, managers, and English himself. Tony Hsieh valued the customer service so much that he built a customer service training program for all new hires regardless of their portfolio. His customer service went to such lengths that his people went to a rival shoe shop to get a pair of shoes which were not available on the website. The point is, always answer the calls, take care of your customers and fix problems when they come in. Your clientele will love you for the service.

6. Affiliate Marketing

It has been around since the days when WWW was introduced and yet it still gets overlooked. However, it is extremely effective in raising brand awareness significantly. With a number of affiliate networks operating out there working on PPC or PPA (Pay Per Action) basis, it has never been safer and easier to find whether your product is actually being promoted by the appropriate publishers. Amazon, eBay, and some other establishments offer their very own affiliate networks however, you may also try for exclusive PPA affiliate networks.

7. Establish Trust in the Community by Publishing Reviews etc.

There are many new and competitive businesses congesting almost all industries. It is getting more and more difficult to stand and grow in terms of a decent following. In order to gain support, organizations must be able to establish trust. There are as many as 88% customers who trust online reviews as much as personal recommendations so it is only sensible to start publishing reviews and sending samples of the product for the trusted bloggers to read and judge.

As the company starts to grow, begin placing in-house content on the large websites which publish syndicated content such as Forbes, Huffington Post, Fast Company Inc., and FT. Do not forget to use your real name here as people respond better to humans rather than corporations.

8. Connect with Influencers

Engage with the large player in the industry as it is an effective method for garnering a wide customer base. As, when you can get the attention of an influencer or a thought leader, you have a better chance of capturing their friends and fans as well as establish credibility and trust. Reach out to the entrepreneurs at conferences or bloggers on Twitter or send them interesting and relevant blog content which may raise their interest and again-be human, not just an organization.

9. Post Content on Blogs

Keep the practice of continuously and diligently posting original and relevant blog content. It keeps your organization shining in the Google. However, it also helps potential customers to know your company truly and know where it is coming from. This content doesn't have to be all self-promoting, rather it should offer context and insight into why the reader should buy the product or service. Suggest the best methods for solving industry-related issues which appear in the everyday life of your customers or impart some useful information and in general inspire people to share your point of view. In case you do not have sufficient writers or resources on the payroll to keep out rolling a constant flow of content on the blog, you can enlist to the content marketing platforms such as Content.ly or virtual communication platforms such as Commeta.

10. Use Newsletters to Foster Leads

One of the most difficult tasks in online marketing is generating leads. Often this involves analyzing the customer information and social media activities, placing ads, online surveys and yearly updating of user data. However, new companies keep coming up to simplify the lead generation and in some cases do the work for you. One example is LeadGenius. For nurturing prospects, a great method is using personalized email newsletters, promotional campaigns, and A/B test advertising. Use data to fine tune the efforts that are showing results and develop the best possible campaign.

Chapter 9: Machine Learning Applications for Marketing

Success at marketing depends on several factors. Apart from those mentioned above the marketers cannot win without mastering automation and data analytics. Machine learning can improve the performance of common tasks such as generating branded collateral, customer segmentation, customer communication, extraction and classification of relevant content, overall productivity and output. In the modern economy marketing companies without machine learning will be operating with a serious handicap. However, adopting ML without understanding what it can do is likely to cause more harm than benefit (normally expressed in terms of wasted hours and money). It is no magic and will not move the needle automatically unless your team chooses and configures the correct ML solution for particular marketing challenges. Here are 14 applications using machine learning techniques for marketing:

1. Customer Segmentation and Discovery by Clustering

All your clientele is not the same. The unsupervised ML can aid you to group the audience into dynamic groups and engage them suitably. For example, Affinio's platform analyses billions of customer interest variables, find the particular customer interests based on their social media activities and then generates visual reports grouping the customers having similar interests. After this, you are able to gain insight on the customer behavior you can identify who is a die-hard foodie, who follows what series on Netflix or who have a liking for similar travel destinations.

2. Content Optimization by using Multi-Arm Contextual Bandits

A/B tests is an effective way of finding out which kind of content (web page layout, email tone, article headlines, and visual elements etc.) resonate better with the audience. But, there is a period of regret in A/B testing where you can lose revenue when you are using less optimal options. You need to wait and finish the countdown till you learn what the best option is. The bandit test, on the other hand, reduces the opportunity loss via dynamic optimization. In the process, it explores and exploits the options simultaneously thereby moving towards the better option gradually and automatically.

3. Regression Models with Dynamic Pricing

The correct pricing can make or break the future of a product. The regression techniques in ML permit the marketers to predict statistical values based on previously existing features. This, in turn, permits them to enhance various aspects of the client's journey. Regression can also be utilized for sales forecasting and optimizing marketing expenditure.

4. Text Classification for Personalization and User Insight

A machine learning system can use NLP (Natural Language Processing) to probe voice or text-based content then classify all pieces of the content based on variables like the sentiment, topic or tone to generate customer insight or curate relevant material. The Tone Analyzer from IBM Watson can parse through the customer feedback from the internet and determine the general tone of users that are reviewing the products.

5. Text Extraction and Summary for Trending News

Machine learning can be leveraged by the marketers to extract relevant content from the news articles published online and other sources of data to determine what the people's views are about their brand and how they react to the products. For this the "Protagonist" platform enables organizations to gain complete visibility of their client's motivations and values and how these attributes can affect their purchasing decisions. The technology savvy marketers can also build their own machine learning algorithms by using APIs like AYLIEN for social media sentiment monitoring and relevant news aggregation among other purposes.

6. Machine Translation Using Attentional Neural Networks

The attention mechanisms of deep learning aid in helping improve the machine translation and enrich your marketing assets for global competition. The translation was a major expenditure for a brand entering into a new and linguistically different market. However, the development in the AI field has enabled machine translation to gain near human parity. In order to rationalize the costs and speed up this process, several companies opt to just have human translators review and sign off the output from machine translation.

7. Text Generation by using RNN (Recurrent Neural Networks)

In case the creative people of your brand are under constant pressure to come up with great names for your newer products and campaigns, you may use generative models such as RNN to serve yourselves with several plausible sounding names. Some could be catchy/weird and some surprisingly the exact ones you need.

8. Dialog System for Chatbots and Automation of Customer Experience

Chatbots and bots are some of the most universal uses of ML. However, most marketing bots you observe in the wild are totally scripted and they use minimal ML and natural language processing. When the dialog systems are more sophisticated, they are able to refer to the external knowledge bases. They can adapt to unusual queries and also escalate to the human bots if required. Many companies these days have adopted the chatbots to communicate with their customers. They stay with the customers' right from when they have just learned about a new product or a brand onto after they have made the buy and need customer support.

9. Voice Based Searching Using TTS and STT

It is considered as a part of conversational AI domain. The voice only or voice-enabled platforms bring a new paradigm and customer engagement possibilities inside the software and hardware interfaces. Due to the rising use of voice-based digital assistants like Google Assistant and Amazon Echo, the touch-free search and shopping are getting enabled. So now the marketers need conversational AI strategies as it is the future of marketing.

10. Brand Object Recognition by using Computer Vision

Computer vision is a rapidly developing area of machine learning that can be lent to a range of applications. Marketers can make use of the machine learning powered vision for recognizing the product and extract the insight from the images on the labels and videos. Solutions such as GumGum permit the marketers to know when their logos have appeared in generated content and quickly calculate the earnings from video analysis. The more technically savvy marketers can make use of APIs such as Clarifai to build customized solutions for moderating content and also for recommendation and search engines which are based on visual similarities.

11. Original Media with GANs (Generative Adversarial Networks)

Nvidia caused a huge uproar in the business community and created a buzz because of its methodology of generating photorealistic images of duplicate celebrities. Although these photos look like images of real people they are not. They are completely generated by ML and AI. By using the GAN (Generative Adversarial Networks) the Nvidia system became progressively more capable of creating ultra-realistic but fake images.

GAN has two competing networks, one is a generator and the second is the discriminator which spar and learn from one another. Thereby they steadily become better at creating and also detecting fake images. Some other companies use GAN for creating logos, making photorealistic images out of sketches and also for generating voices.

12. Automation of Robotic Processes for Marketing Operations

Digital marketing is full of automated solutions aimed at making work operations easier for hard-pressed workers. Automated processes exist for opening and analyzing email attachments, reading emails, data entry for template reports and engaging and tracking social media triggers to allow the marketers to stay ahead on the curve. For the ads on the internet, there is an AI platform called "Albert" who decreases the human need for large-scale purchase of media, hastening the speed of necessary analytical computations and optimizing the paid advertisement campaigns.

13. Superior Reporting by Using Automated Data Visualization

Images speak better than words. AI is quicker and more efficient at transferring data to visual insights than any human experts. The human analysts normally use tools such as Tableau or Excel to create virtual representations manually. However, the automated analytical solutions intended for businesses like Qlik can centralize the data sources to generate meaningful reports and dashboards for the marketing teams. Several platforms these days use data analytics with sophisticated machine learning algorithms to vividly clarify market trends. The behavior pattern of customers and other data that is hidden otherwise from plain viewing. This data is not easily available for conversion into practical insights.

14. Sequential Marketing Decisions Using Reinforcement Learning

Many of the difficult decisions we make are not singular predictions and they are a series of decisions taken over a long period of time. Balancing the short-term trade-offs to the long-term benefits is tough for even smartest humans. The reinforcement learning is used successfully in DeepMind's AlphaGo to beat human decision making in case of complex scenarios. Although the business scenarios are far more complex than games, the success in case of smaller domains suggests similar progress in the larger ones. The IBM researchers conducted a notable study to explore the possibility of the use of reinforcement learning to improve targeted marketing.

Chapter 10: Machine Learning Applications for Finance

ML had useful applications in finance even before the advancement of efficient chatbots, mobile banking apps, and search engines. Due to the high volumes, the requirement of the accuracy of historical records and the quantitative nature of the world of finance, very few other industries are more suited for artificial intelligence. You can find more cases of the use of machine learning in finance sector than ever before. It is a trend accentuated by greater computing power and more accessible ML tools such as Google's TensorFlow. ML has arrived and plays a crucial role in modern society and in many areas of finance. It is involved in approving loans, managing assets and assessing risks. Although very few tech-savvy people have an accurate view of how many views are there in which ML finds its way in the financial lives of people.

Here are some examples of ML being put to use in today's world. Keep in mind that some of the applications use multiple AI technologies or approaches and not just ML.

1. Portfolio Management

Robo-Advisor is a term not heard of a few years ago but is now used commonly in the financial world. The term, however, is a little misleading as it doesn't involve any robots at all. Instead, the Robo-advisors (e.g. Betterment or Wealthfront) are algorithms based on ML and built to shape the financial portfolio of a user including their goals and risk tolerance. For example, users enter goals such as retiring at the age of 65 with $3, 00,000 in saving. They also enter their age, current financial status, and income.

The advisor who can be more accurately referred to as an allocator then spends the investments across assets classes and financial instruments to arrive at the user's goals. The advisor system then calibrates to the changes in user's goals and to the actual changes in the market thereby finding the best fit for the user's goals. They have gained significant importance among consumers that do not need physical advisors to feel comfortable in investments and those who are incapable of paying fees to human advisors.

2. Trading with Algorithms

Algorithm trading goes as far back as the 1970s and is also called automated trading systems. It makes use of difficult AI systems to agree on very fast trading decisions. The algorithmic systems make thousands or millions of trades in one day. Therefore the term HFT (High-Frequency Trading) is used and it is a part of algorithmic trading. Most of the financial institutions and hedge funds don't disclose their AI approach they are using for trading. However, it is believed that deep learning and ML are playing a rising important role in trading decisions. There are some exceptional limitations to the use of ML in trading stocks.

3. Detecting Frauds

The Internet is finding a common use these days with its computing powers and more companies are using it to store valuable organization data online and yet this is a perfect case for the data security risk. Although previous financial fraud detection systems relied mostly on the robust and complex set of rules, the modern fraud detection goes beyond following a checklist of different risk factors. It actually learns and makes provisions for new and potential security threats. This is the reason for the presence of ML in fraud detection. The same principles are true for all data security problems. The system can detect abnormal behavior or unique activities by using machine learning and flag them to the security department. The main challenge for this system is to avoid false positives and situations where risks get flagged when actually there aren't any. There are a high number of ways in which security can get breached so genuine learning systems will become a necessity in coming 5 to 10 years.

4. Insurance or Loan Underwriting

Underwriting can be described as the perfect job for ML in finance but there is a lot of worry in the market that the machines will replace many of underwriting positions in existence today. Especially in large organizations such as large banks and public limited insurance companies, the ML algorithms can be trained on millions of instances of consumer data such as jobs, age, marital status etc. It can also be used for insurance results and financial lending in checking whether a person defaulted or not or is paying his loans on time or has been involved in a car accident.

The underlying trends can be assessed by using algorithms and analyzed constantly to detect trends which influence lending and insurance for the future. For example, you can find whether more and more youngsters are getting into car accidents. Or is there an increasing rate of defaults among a specific demography in the last 10 years? The results of these queries have a great yield for the organizations. However, this is limited at the moment to large companies having the resources to get data scientists and possessing the massive amount of data (past and present) to train the algorithms.

5. Machine Learning and Cryptocurrencies

The AI and machine learning assisted trading has attracted huge interest in the last few years. There is a hypothesis that the inefficiencies in the cryptocurrency markets can be used to create large profits. The normal trading strategies helped by the state of the art ML algorithms are far more capable than the standard benchmarks. Some nontrivial but actually simple algorithms can aid in anticipating the short-term evolution of cryptocurrencies market.

The success that ML techniques had with the predictions of stock markets suggested that the methods could be used effectively to predict the cryptocurrency prices as well. But applying the ML algorithm to the cryptocurrency market is limited mainly to analyzing the Bitcoin prices by using the Bayesian neural network, random forests, long and short-term memory neural networks and some other algorithms. These studies anticipated to a degree the price fluctuations of Bitcoin and concluded that the best results could be achieved by using algorithms that were based on neural networks. The reinforcement deep learning was able to beat the performance of buy and hold strategies in predicting the prices of 12 different cryptocurrencies over a period of one year. There were other attempts to use ML for predicting prices of cryptocurrencies other than Bitcoin however they came from non-academic resources and did not provide comparisons for the results.

6. Day Trading with Machine Learning

The speculation in securities is called as day trading. More specifically it refers to buying and selling financial instruments on the same day of trading. Strictly speaking, it is a trading happening within a single day. It means that all positions get closed when the market is closed for the day. The day traders look at identifying the entry and exit positions on the stocks that have favorable conditions. These conditions yield several small term profits that can add up to big gains.

In case there are people in the market who can recognize favorable patterns in the market than we can train even a machine to perform similarly and even at superhuman levels. This is the goal of using machine learning for day trading. But first, we need to identify the strategies used by day traders to signal entry conditions in the market. The technique is split into two processes, the first is a high-level pattern description and the second is machine learning.

In the first process, we just look at identifying entry semantics which occurs for possibly hundreds of predefined strategies. This is done by using robust and highly scalable pattern matchers such as Apache Flink. Once a pattern has been triggered we can go through the historical data and find the instances in the past when patterns were triggered and there was the outcome price after 10 or 20 minutes. We can generate a training example for the algorithms where we use machine learning for creating probability distribution about the past entries.

Chapter 11: The Future of AI and Machine Learning

There is no doubt about the fact that ML is a revolutionary technology. It is also a critical aspect of many new and established companies. Wei Lei the VP and GM of Intel opines that ML is becoming more and more sophisticated with passing years and we have not seen its full potential yet. This may go beyond self-driving cars, retail trends analysis or fraud detection devices. So what is the future of machine learning and how will it impact the world? Here are some forecasts:

1. Better Unsupervised algorithms

Unsupervised algorithms are used in ML to predict using data sets when just the input data is available without the corresponding output variables. In supervised ML the output is already known. The unsupervised ML is really closely related with the real AI. The whole concept that the machines can learn and identify complex patterns and processes without any apparent human intervention. When the algorithm is left alone to research and present useful patterns from the datasets you can discover hidden patterns or groupings which would have been difficult to extract using just the supervised ML method. In the upcoming times, we will see improvements in the unsupervised ML algorithms. The development of better algorithms will result in quicker and more accurate ML predictions.

2. Improved Personalization

The ML personalization algorithms are utilized to offer recommendations to the users and entice them into completing certain actions. By using these algorithms you can synthesize the patterns in the data and arrive at suitable conclusions such as the realization of one's personal interests. For example, the algorithms can judge from a person's browsing activities on some retail site on the internet and find out that he has an interest in buying a mower for his garden. Without this insight, buyers might leave the site without actually making the purchase. However many of these recommendations today are annoying and inaccurate thereby crippling the user experience. But in the future, the personalization algorithms will become fine-tuned and so leading towards a more successful and satisfactory experience.

3. Raised Use of Quantum Computing

The quantum ML algorithms have the potential to change the field of ML. These algorithms, for example, can use the benefits of quantum computation to improve the capabilities of classic ML techniques. In case Quantum Computers are integrated into ML, it will lead to quicker data processing and will accelerate the ML capability to synthesize data and draw insights. That is what the future holds for customers and humans as a whole.

The quantum powered systems can provide a quicker and more heavy-duty computation for both supervised and unsupervised algorithms. This enhanced performance will lead to the unlocking of many ML possibilities which may not have been visualized during the times of classic computers.

4. Enhanced Cognitive Services

The cognitive services contain a set of ML APIs, SDKs, and services that allow the developers to add intellectual capabilities in their applications. These services can be used by the developers to enable their applications to carry out different duties like speech detection, vision recognition, and speech understanding. As technology continues to develop we will see the creation of very intelligent applications which can see, hear, speak and even reason with the surrounding entities. Therefore the researchers will be able to develop more engaging and inquisitive applications which will be able to interpret the user's needs based on normal communication techniques.

5. The Rise of Machines (Robots)

With the sophistication of machine learning enhancing continuously we can see raised use of robots. Robots depend on ML for accomplishing different tasks. Capabilities such as self-supervised learning, robot vision, and multi-agent learning are just around the corner. We can expect the robots to become better at accomplishing these tasks. We will see increased use of robots and drones in manufacturing and other kinds of robots are likely to be utilized more to make human life easier.

6. Impact of ML/AI on Employment and Verticals

Even though AI improves our world dramatically in many ways you can find some concerns regarding its impact on workforce and employment. There are predictions about millions of unemployed people in the coming decades primarily due to the implementation of AI and intelligent automation. In any event, the whole socio-economic system is entering a transformation phase. But businesses, markets, education, governments, social welfare, and employment models are going to be severely affected.

Jobs at Risk

It is easy to automate the monotonous tasks and this will slowly make certain roles obsolete. For example, the activities and tasks of call center or support operations, discovery and retrieval, document classification and content moderation will become more and more dependent on technology and automation with less and less requirement of human work. Same is true for operations and production lines support. Humans are being replaced by smart robots who can navigate safely in the space, can find and move objects such as tools, parts or products and can even perform difficult assembly operations.

In the longer run, we will see some of the jobs and roles becoming less and less relevant and then obsolete. However, in most cases AI and ML will have supporting roles to the humans, enabling them to perform better in handling critical and difficult situations that require creative thinking and judgment? However, in the same vein, there will be many new roles and specialties generated which will be in sync with technology and science. For example, there will be a need for skilled professionals to manage AI training programs to make sure that the systems are proper in terms of security, integrity, proper use and objectivity. Although many verticals will be affected, there will be a host of new business opportunities which will empower the culture of creativeness, entrepreneurship and innovation.

Chapter 12: Conclusion

Because of the unique benefits of machine learning especially on the small devices, it is clearly becoming a favorite with businesses. From RPA functions to mobile automation it is all becoming a handheld reality bringing the future into the palm of your hands. Nowadays even the smaller businesses can leverage ML like the bigger boys. It can be used in cost-effective ways. For example, some companies use AI for improving customer relations. It reduces the costs and at the same time provides customized assistance to their companies. It can also be utilized to train the workforce and to improve forecasting cost-effectively. For example, Udacity which is an educational institution enhanced their sales by 50% by introducing chatbots to their sales teams. The advancements in data, algorithms and infrastructure and the costs required for getting them has decreased their overall costing and nowadays smaller businesses can afford them.

However, there are a host of questions raised about ethics in relation to machine learning. Systems that are trained on data sets with biases might lead to digitalization of cultural prejudices. For example, using data from a job hiring firm with racist policies will lead to machine learning systems duplicating the bias during the selection of applicants. Collecting "responsible data" and proper documentation of rules for algorithms to be used by systems has become significant. Even the languages contain biases and ML will have to learn them. Healthcare professionals developing the machines for generating income rather than serving people is another concern. There are some shining advantages as well. As AI will increase productivity in many jobs although lower and middle-level positions will get eliminated. In its position, several new positions with highly skilled, medium skilled and even low skilled range of people will be required.

Algorithm Example: Hotel Recommendation Engine Using Machine Learning

Most travel agencies operating online are scrambling to meet the personalization standards set by Netflix and Amazon. These are artificial intelligence driven standards and the online travel agencies are becoming highly competitive with various brands trying to capture the client's attention and money by comparing, recommending, sharing and matching. In this case study we aim at creating optimal hotel recommendations for the Expedia clients which are searching for hotels. This problem will be modelled as a multi-class classification problem and we will build SVM and a decision tree in an ensemble method and predict which cluster of hotels the guest is likely to book given his search criteria.

The data provided is anonymized and all the fields well almost all are in numeric formats. The data set may be found at Kaggle. We use train.csv in this case which captures the logs of client behavior and we will also use destinations.csv which contains all the information pertaining to the hotel reviews made by the clients. The figure below gives the schema of train.csv:

Feature Name	Feature Description	Feature Data Type
date_time	Timestamp	string
site_name	ID of Expedia point of sale	int
posa_continent	ID of continent associate with site name	int
user_location_country	the ID of the country the user is located	int
user_location_region	the ID of the region the user is located	int
user_location_city	the ID of the city the user is located	int
orig_destination_distance	physical distance between a hotel and a customer at the time of search	double
user_id	ID of user	int
is_mobile	1 when a user connected from a mobile device, 0 otherwise	tinyint
is_package	1 if the click/booking was generated as part of a package, 0 otherwise	int
channel	ID of a marketing channel	int
srch_ci	Checkin date	string
srch_co	Checkout date	string
srch_adults_cnt	The number of adults specified in the hotel room	int
srch_children_cnt	The number of children specified in the hotel room	int
srch_rm_cnt	The number of hotel rooms specified in the search	int
srch_destination_id	ID of the destination where the hotel search was performed	int
srch_destination_type_id	Type of destination	int
hotel_continent	Hotel continent	int
hotel_country	Hotel country	int
hotel_market	Hotel market	int
cnt	Number of similar events in the context of the same user session	int
is_booking	1 if a booking, 0 if a click	int
hotel_cluster	ID of a hotel cluster - *This is what we are going to predict*	bigint

The next figure gives the schema of destinations.csv:

Feature Name	Feature Description	Feature Data Type
srch_destination_id	ID of the destination where the hotel search was performed	int
d1-d149	latent description of search regions	double

import datetime

import pandas as pd

import numpy as np

import matplotlib.pyplot as plt

import seaborn as sns

%matplotlib inline

from sklearn.model_selection import cross_val_score

from sklearn.ensemble import RandomForestClassifier

from sklearn.pipeline import make_pipeline

from sklearn import preprocessing

from sklearn.preprocessing import StandardScaler

from sklearn import svm

In order to process at a local level we sampled just the 1% of the total records. After which there is still a large number of records remaining at 241, 179.

df = pd.read_csv('train.csv.gz', sep=',').dropna()

dest = pd.read_csv('destinations.csv.gz')

df = df.sample(frac=0.01, random_state=99)

df.shape

The objective in this case is to guess which hotel_cluster the client will book from the information he has provided in the search. Here there are a total of 100 clusters. In proper terms, we are dealing with a problem which is 100 class classification.

```
plt.figure(figsize=(12, 6))
sns.distplot(df['hotel_cluster'])
```

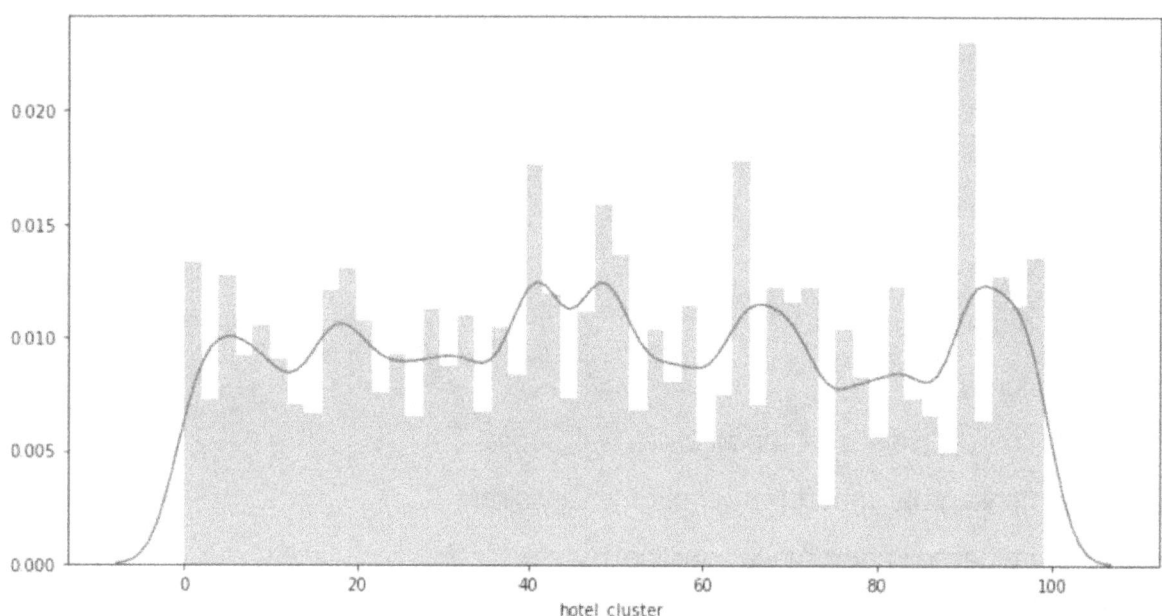

As you can see the data is well distributed across the 100 clusters and there is the presence of skewness in this data.

Feature Engineering

The time, date, check-in and check-out date columns cannot be utilized directly. We will extract the month and year out of them. First let us define a few functions to achieve this and then we will define a function to merge with the destination.csv.

```
from datetime import datetime
def get_year(x):
    if x is not None and type(x) is not float:
        try:
            return datetime.strptime(x, '%Y-%m-%d').year
```

```
        except ValueError:
            return datetime.strptime(x, '%Y-%m-%d %H:%M:%S').year
    else:
return 2013
        pass


def get_month(x):
    if x is not None and type(x) is not float:
        try:
            return datetime.strptime(x, '%Y-%m-%d').month
        except:
            return datetime.strptime(x, '%Y-%m-%d %H:%M:%S').month
    else:
        return 1
        pass


def left_merge_dataset(left_dframe, right_dframe, merge_column):
    return pd.merge(left_dframe, right_dframe, on=merge_column, how='left')
```

Treating the date_time column:

```
df['date_time_year'] = pd.Series(df.date_time, index = df.index)
df['date_time_month'] = pd.Series(df.date_time, index = df.index)
from datetime import datetime
df.date_time_year = df.date_time_year.apply(lambda x: get_year(x))
df.date_time_month = df.date_time_month.apply(lambda x: get_month(x))
del df['date_time']
```

Treating the srch_ci column:

```
df['srch_ci_year'] = pd.Series(df.srch_ci, index=df.index)
df['srch_ci_month'] = pd.Series(df.srch_ci, index=df.index)
# convert year & months to int
df.srch_ci_year = df.srch_ci_year.apply(lambda x: get_year(x))
df.srch_ci_month = df.srch_ci_month.apply(lambda x: get_month(x))
# remove the srch_ci column
del df['srch_ci']
```

Treating the srch_co column:

```
df['srch_co_year'] = pd.Series(df.srch_co, index=df.index)
df['srch_co_month'] = pd.Series(df.srch_co, index=df.index)
# convert year & months to int
df.srch_co_year = df.srch_co_year.apply(lambda x: get_year(x))
df.srch_co_month = df.srch_co_month.apply(lambda x: get_month(x))
# remove the srch_co column
del df['srch_co']
```

Preliminary Analysis

After the creation of new features and removal of features that are not so useful, we wanted to know if anything relates well to the hotel_cluster. This tells us if we need to pay more attention to some specific features.

```
df.corr()["hotel_cluster"].sort_values()
```

```
srch_destination_type_id     -0.036120
site_name                    -0.027497
hotel_country                -0.023837
is_booking                   -0.022898
user_location_country        -0.020239
srch_destination_id          -0.016736
srch_co_month                -0.005874
srch_rm_cnt                  -0.005570
srch_ci_month                -0.005015
date_time_month              -0.002142
channel                      -0.001386
date_time_year               -0.000435
cnt                           0.000378
hotel_continent               0.000422
user_location_city            0.001241
user_id                       0.003891
orig_destination_distance     0.006084
user_location_region          0.006927
srch_ci_year                  0.008562
is_mobile                     0.008788
srch_co_year                  0.009287
posa_continent                0.012180
srch_adults_cnt               0.012407
srch_children_cnt             0.014901
hotel_market                  0.022149
is_package                    0.047598
hotel_cluster                 1.000000
Name: hotel_cluster, dtype: float64
```

As we can see, there is no column that relates linearly with the hotel_cluster. This means that the methods that model linear relationship between the features may not be suitable for this issue.

Strategy

If you make a quick Google search it is easy to learn that for known combinations of different search destinations, hotel country or hotel market you will find the necessary hotel cluster. Let's do this.

pieces = [df.groupby(['srch_destination_id','hotel_country','hotel_market','hotel_cluster'])['is_booking'].agg(['sum','count'])]
agg = pd.concat(pieces).groupby(level=[0,1,2,3]).sum()
agg.dropna(inplace=True)
agg.head()

srch_destination_id	hotel_country	hotel_market	hotel_cluster	sum	count
4	7	246	22	0	1
			29	0	1
			30	0	1
			32	1	2
			43	0	1

agg['sum_and_cnt'] = 0.85*agg['sum'] + 0.15*agg['count']
agg = agg.groupby(level=[0,1,2]).apply(lambda x: x.astype(float)/x.sum())
agg.reset_index(inplace=True)
agg.head()

	srch_destination_id	hotel_country	hotel_market	hotel_cluster	sum	count	sum_and_cnt
0	4	7	246	22	0.0	0.125	0.073171
1	4	7	246	29	0.0	0.125	0.073171
2	4	7	246	30	0.0	0.125	0.073171
3	4	7	246	32	1.0	0.250	0.560976
4	4	7	246	43	0.0	0.125	0.073171

```
agg_pivot = agg.pivot_table(index=['srch_destination_id','hotel_country','hotel_market'],
columns='hotel_cluster', values='sum_and_cnt').reset_index()
agg_pivot.head()
```

hotel_cluster	srch_destination_id	hotel_country	hotel_market	0	1	2	3	4	5	6	...	90	91	92	93	94	95	96	97
0	4	7	246	NaN	NaN	NaN	NaN	NaN	NaN	NaN	...	NaN	NaN	NaN	NaN	NaN	NaN	NaN	NaN
1	8	50	416	NaN	NaN	NaN	NaN	NaN	NaN	NaN	...	NaN	0.025210	NaN	NaN	NaN	NaN	NaN	NaN
2	11	50	824	NaN	NaN	NaN	NaN	NaN	NaN	NaN	...	NaN	NaN	NaN	NaN	NaN	NaN	NaN	NaN
3	14	27	1434	NaN	NaN	NaN	NaN	NaN	NaN	NaN	...	NaN	NaN	NaN	NaN	NaN	NaN	NaN	NaN
4	16	50	419	NaN	NaN	NaN	NaN	NaN	NaN	NaN	...	NaN	0.344828	NaN	NaN	NaN	NaN	NaN	NaN

5 rows × 103 columns

Merge this with our destination table and the latest creation of aggregate pivot table.

```
df = pd.merge(df, dest, how='left', on='srch_destination_id')
df = pd.merge(df, agg_pivot, how='left',
on=['srch_destination_id','hotel_country','hotel_market'])
df.fillna(0, inplace=True)
df.shape
```

Implementing the Algorithms

We are basically interested in booking the events.

```
df = df.loc[df['is_booking'] == 1]
```

Get the features and labels.

```
X = df.drop(['user_id', 'hotel_cluster', 'is_booking'], axis=1)
y = df.hotel_cluster
```

Naïve Bayes

```
from sklearn.naive_bayes import GaussianNB
clf = make_pipeline(preprocessing.StandardScaler(), GaussianNB(priors=None))
np.mean(cross_val_score(clf, X, y, cv=10))
```

0.10347912437041926

K-Nearest Neighbors Classifier

```
from sklearn.neighbors import KNeighborsClassifier
clf = make_pipeline(preprocessing.StandardScaler(), KNeighborsClassifier(n_neighbors=5))
np.mean(cross_val_score(clf, X, y, cv=10, scoring='accuracy'))
```

0.25631461834732266

We reported performance measurement by using k-fold cross-validation and composing estimators was made easy by Pipeline.

```
clf = make_pipeline(preprocessing.StandardScaler(),
RandomForestClassifier(n_estimators=273,max_depth=10,random_state=0))
np.mean(cross_val_score(clf, X, y, cv=10))
```
0.24865023372782996

Multi-class Logistic Regression

```
from sklearn.linear_model import LogisticRegression
```

```
clf = make_pipeline(preprocessing.StandardScaler(), LogisticRegression(multi_class='ovr'))
np.mean(cross_val_score(clf, X, y, cv=10))
```

0.30445543572367767

SVM Classifier

It is pretty time consuming. But we were able to achieve greater results.

```
from sklearn import svm
clf = make_pipeline(preprocessing.StandardScaler(),
svm.SVC(decision_function_shape='ovo'))
np.mean(cross_val_score(clf, X, y, cv=10))
```

0.3228727137315005

After all it looked as if more work was needed in the area of feature engineering in order to improve the results. Source code is available at Github.

Algorithm Example: Customer Segmentation by using Clustering Algorithms

In the modern competitive world it is critical to understand the client behavior and categorize them based on their buying behavior and demography. This is a crucial part of customer segmentation which allows the marketers to focus their marketing efforts better on different audiences in terms of product development, marketing, and promotional strategies.

This case study will demonstrate the concept of customer segmentation data set from e-commerce sites by using k-means clustering of Python. This data set consists of annual income of around 300 clients and their annual expenditure on e-commerce sites. We will make use of k-means clustering algorithm for deriving the maximum number of clusters and understand their underlying customer segments based on the information provided.

Data Set

The data set contain the annual income information of 303 customers in $000 and their total spending in $000 on e-commerce sites over a period of one year. Let's explore this data by using pandas and numpy libraries available in Python.

#Load the required packages
import numpy as np

```python
import pandas as pd
import matplotlib.pyplot as plt
```

#Plot styling

```python
import seaborn as sns; sns.set()  # for plot styling
%matplotlib inline
plt.rcParams['figure.figsize'] = (16, 9)
plt.style.use('ggplot')
```

#Read the csv file

```python
dataset=pd.read_csv('CLV.csv')
```

#Explore the dataset

```python
dataset.head()#top 5 columns
len(dataset) # of rows
```

#descriptive statistics of the dataset

```python
dataset.describe().transpose()
```

	INCOME	SPEND
0	233	150
1	250	187
2	204	172
3	236	178
4	354	163

```python
dataset.head()
```

	count	mean	std	min	25%	50%	75%	max
INCOME	303.0	245.273927	48.499412	126.0	211.0	240.0	274.0	417.0
SPEND	303.0	149.646865	22.905161	71.0	133.5	153.0	166.0	202.0

dataset.describe().transpose()

Data Visualization

The set of data contains 303 rows. The average annual income is 245000 and the mean annual expenditure is 149000. This distribution of annual income and expenditure has been illustrated with a "violinplot" and "distplot". These two provide an inclination towards the data distribution of income and expenditure.

#Visualizing the data - displot

```
plot_income = sns.distplot(dataset["INCOME"])
plot_spend = sns.distplot(dataset["SPEND"])
plt.xlabel('Income / spend')
```

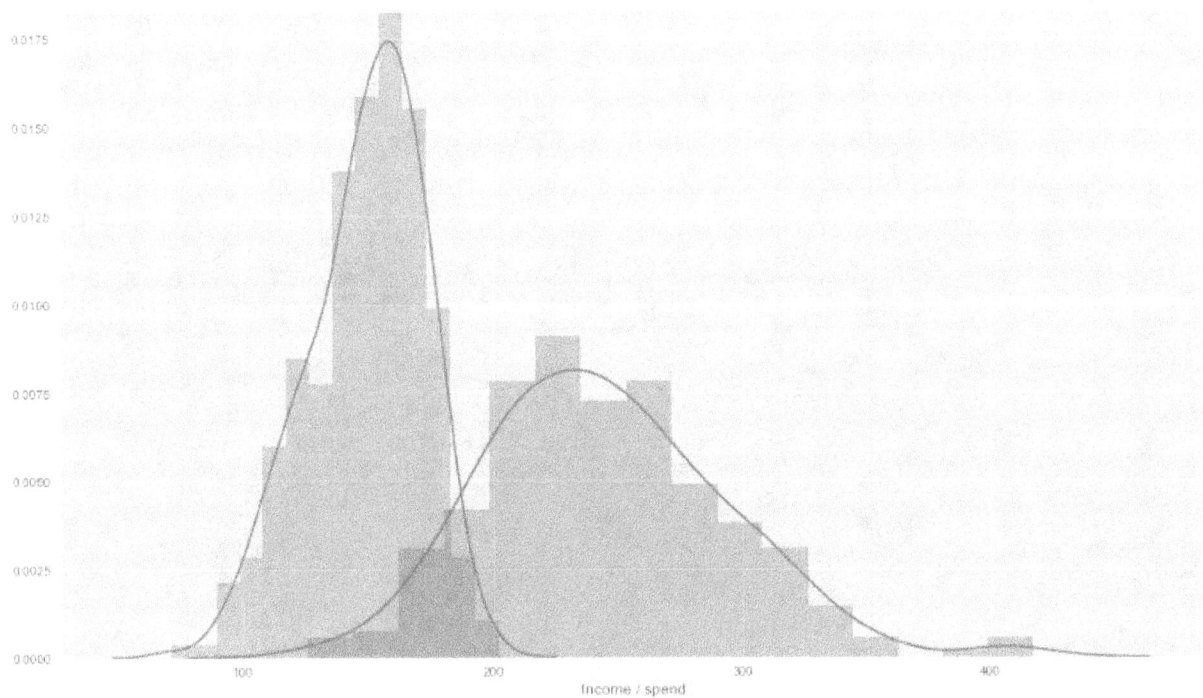

Income and Expenditure Distribution Plot

#Violin plot of Income and Spend

f, axes = plt.subplots(1,2, figsize=(12,6), sharex=True, sharey=True)

v1 = sns.violinplot(data=dataset, x='INCOME', color="skyblue",ax=axes[0])

v2 = sns.violinplot(data=dataset, x='SPEND',color="lightgreen", ax=axes[1])

v1.set(xlim=(0,420))

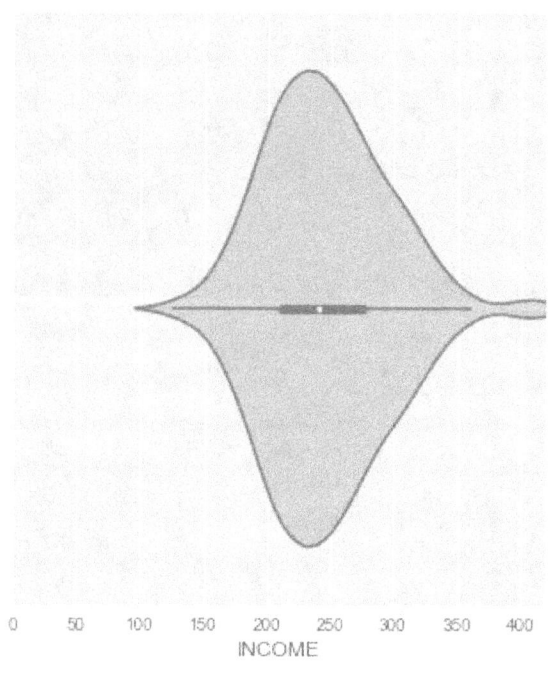 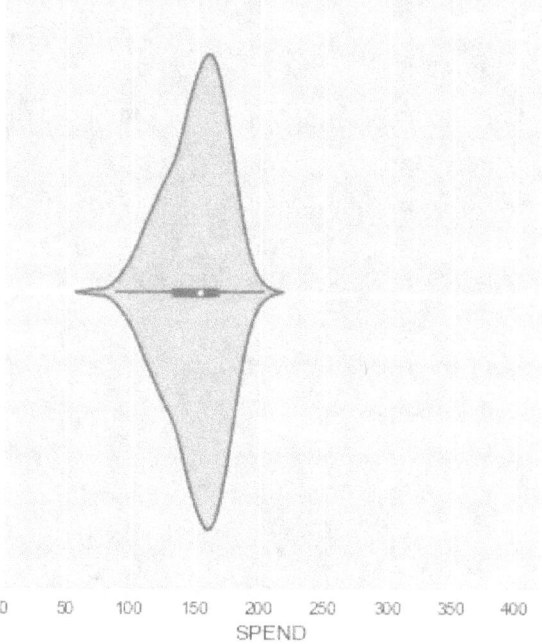

Clustering the Fundamentals

Clustering is an unsupervised kind of machine learning technique where there are no defined independent and dependent variables. The patterns in the information are utilized to identify and group similar patterns.

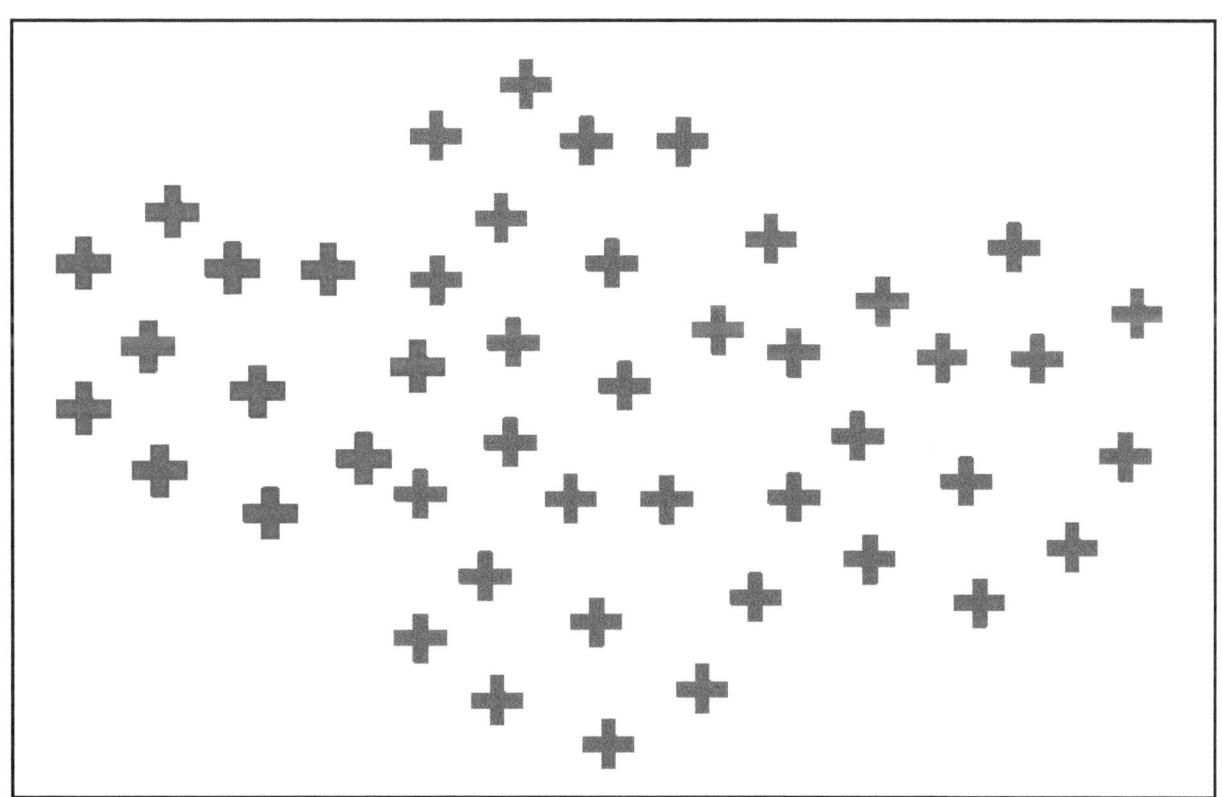
Original dataset

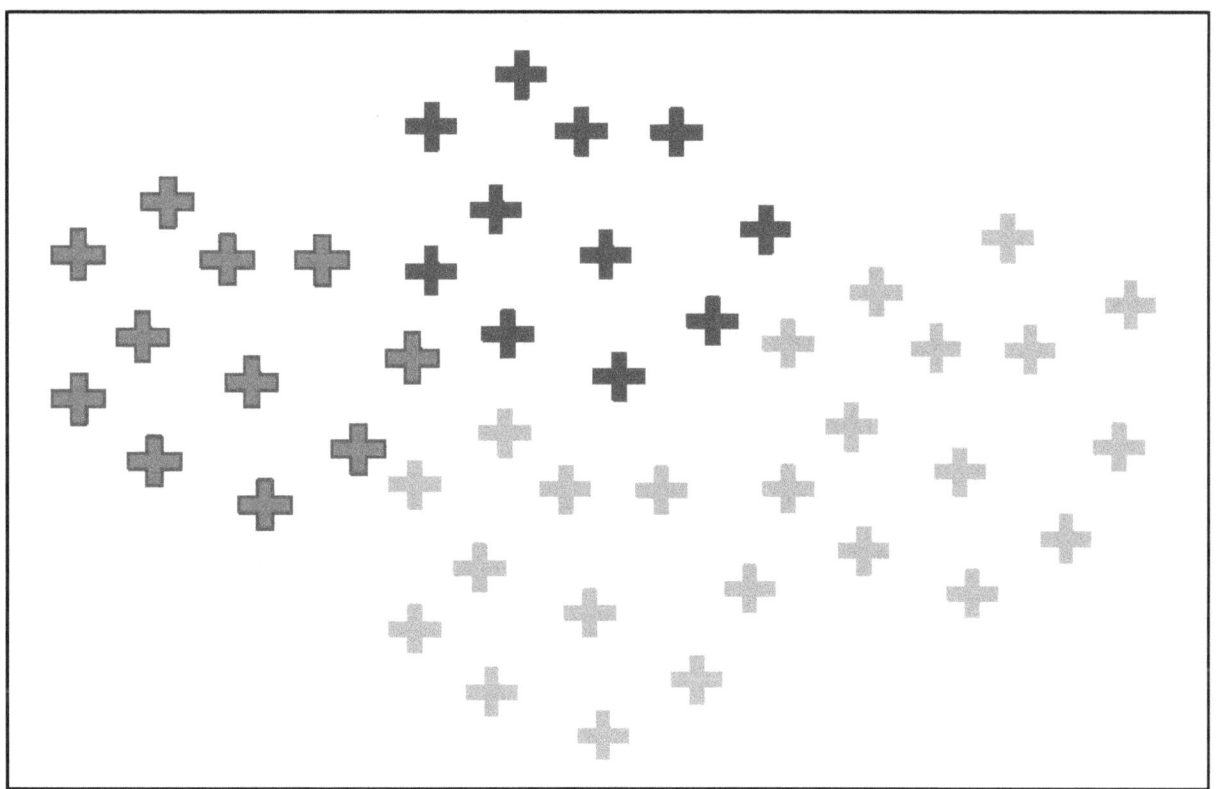
After Clustering

The aim of a clustering algorithm is to make sure that the distance between data points inside the cluster is quite low than compared to the distance between two clusters. In other words, group members are to be quite similar and members of various groups are to be dissimilar. We are going to use k-means clustering for creating customer segments based on their income and expenditure information. The number of clusters K in a K-means clustering algorithm are predetermined and it is an iterative algorithm. So the algorithm iteratively assigns every data point to one of the K clusters and it is based on similarity in features. The basic steps by the K-means algorithm are:

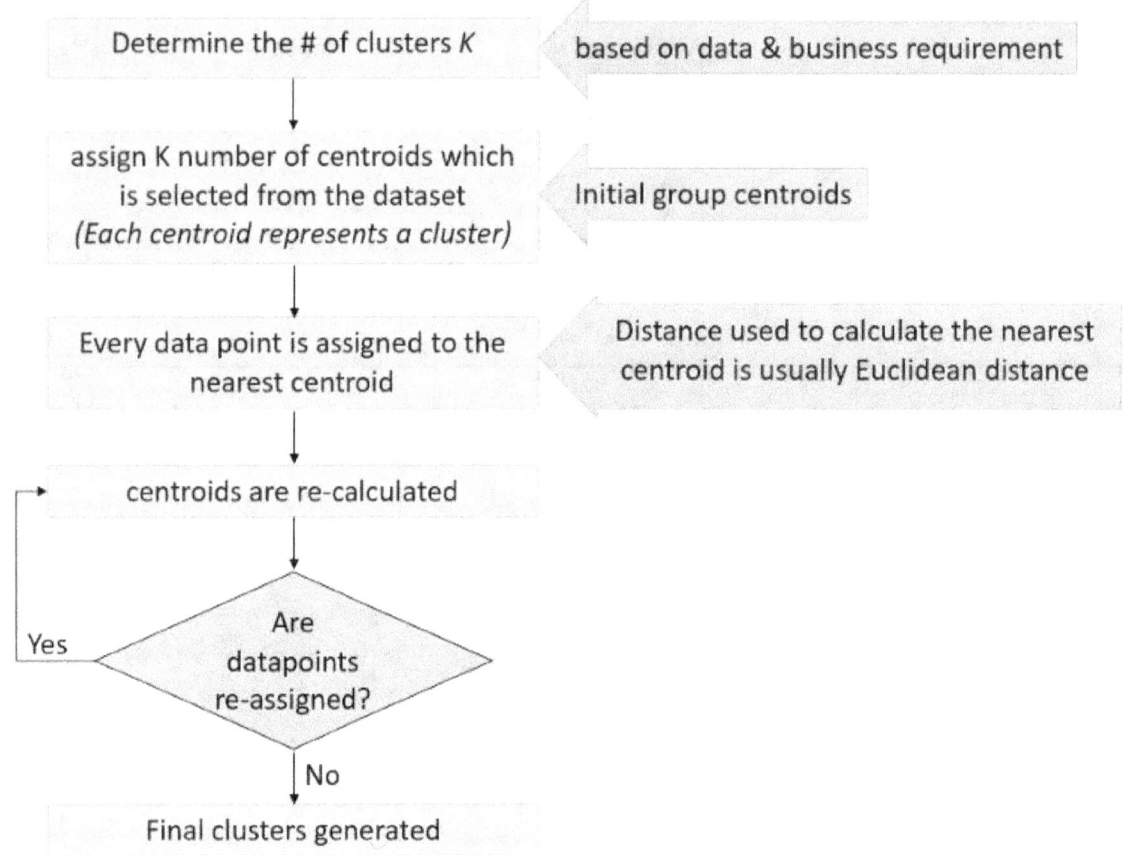

Clustering Mathematics

There is mathematics in the clustering and in simple terms it is minimizing the sum of square of distances between the associated data points of cluster centroid and the cluster centroid itself.

$$Minimize \sum_{j=1}^{k} \sum_{i=1}^{n} (x_{ij} - c_j)^2$$

K = number of clusters.

N = number of data points.

C = centroid of cluster j.

(x_{ij} − c_j)– Distance between data point and centroid to which it is assigned.

Decision regarding the numbers of clusters K:

The number of clusters is main input for the k-means clustering. This figure is derived by using the concept of minimization within cluster sum of square (WCSS). There is a screen plot created that plots number of clusters on the X axis for every cluster number on the Y axis.

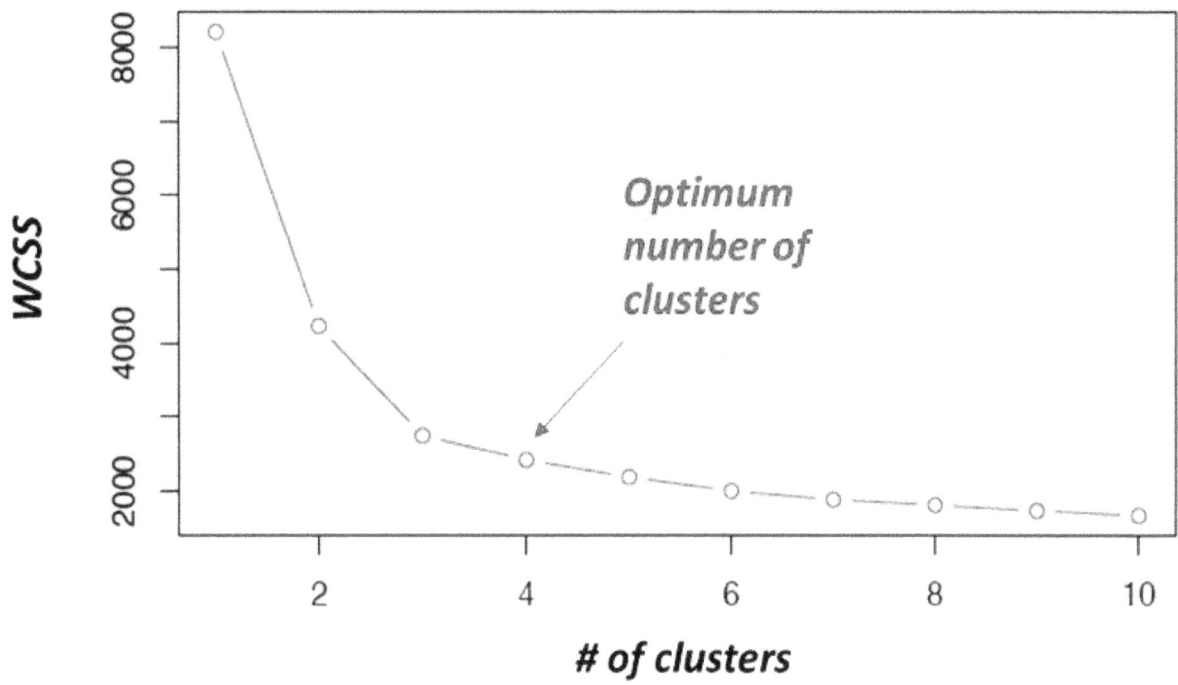

Scree plot / Elbow method to determine optimum number of clusters

With a rise in the number of clusters, the WCSS decreases. This decrease in the WCSS is steep initially and later this rate slows down and an elbow plot emerges as a result. The number of clusters in the elbow formation normally provide an indication about the optimum number of clusters. This together with a specific knowledge of business requirements needs to be used to decide the optimum number of clusters required. For our dataset we arrived at the figure for the optimum number of clusters by using the elbow method.

#Using the elbow method to find the optimum number of clusters

```
from sklearn.cluster import KMeans
wcss = []
for i in range(1,11):
    km=KMeans(n_clusters=i,init='k-means++', max_iter=300, n_init=10, random_state=0)
    km.fit(X)
    wcss.append(km.inertia_)
plt.plot(range(1,11),wcss)
plt.title('Elbow Method')
plt.xlabel('Number of clusters')
plt.ylabel('wcss')
plt.show()
```

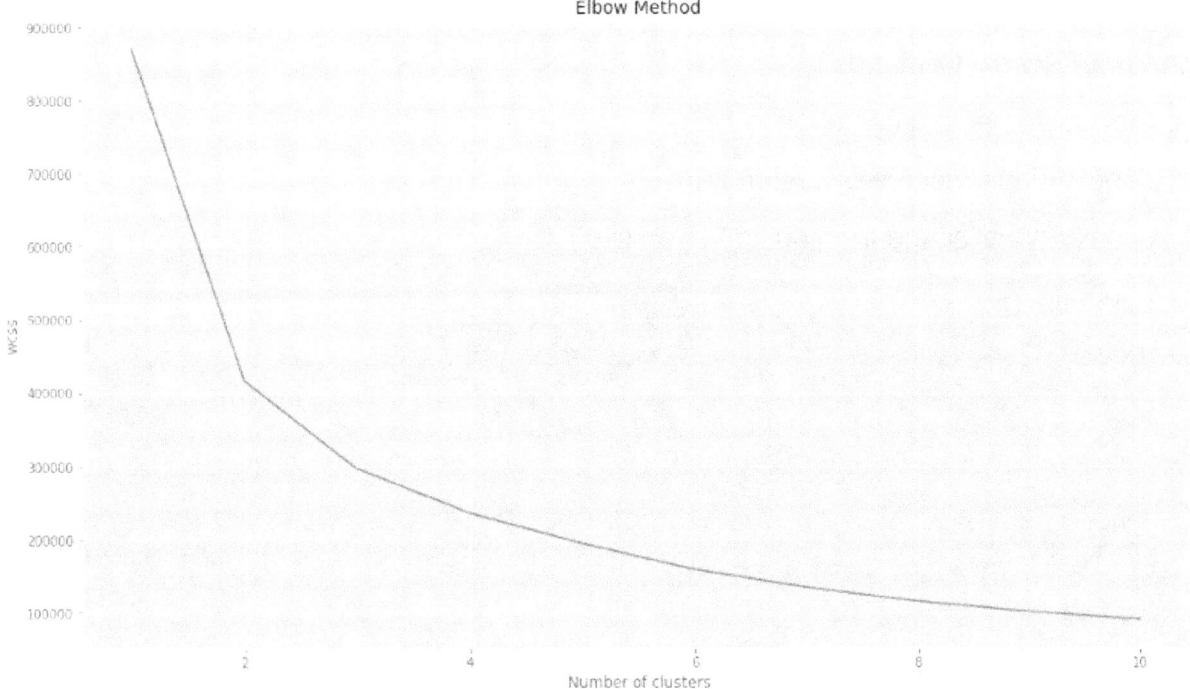

Scree plot of given data set on customer Income & Spend

We could select 4, 5, or 6 clusters based on the information generated by the elbow plot. Let's try both, the actual number of clusters and visualizing the clusters to decide the final number of clusters.

Fitting the k-means clustering to the dataset by using k=4:

#Fitting kmeans to the dataset with k=4

km4=KMeans(n_clusters=4,init='k-means++', max_iter=300, n_init=10, random_state=0)
y_means = km4.fit_predict(X)

#Visualizing the clusters for k=4

plt.scatter(X[y_means==0,0],X[y_means==0,1],s=50, c='purple',label='Cluster1')
plt.scatter(X[y_means==1,0],X[y_means==1,1],s=50, c='blue',label='Cluster2')
plt.scatter(X[y_means==2,0],X[y_means==2,1],s=50, c='green',label='Cluster3')
plt.scatter(X[y_means==3,0],X[y_means==3,1],s=50, c='cyan',label='Cluster4')

plt.scatter(km4.cluster_centers_[:,0], km4.cluster_centers_[:,1],s=200,marker='s', c='red', alpha=0.7, label='Centroids')

plt.title('Customer segments')

plt.xlabel('Annual income of customer')

plt.ylabel('Annual spend from customer on site')

plt.legend()

plt.show()

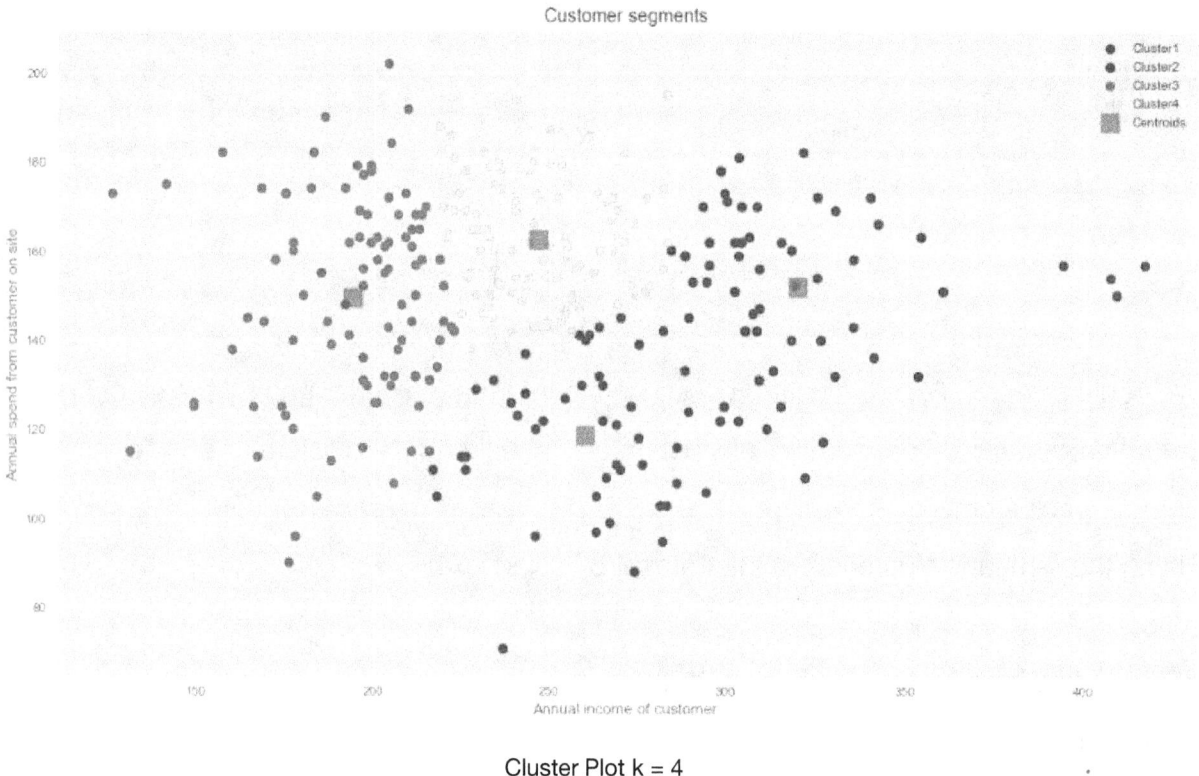

Cluster Plot k = 4

This plot shows a distribution of 4 clusters. They can be interpreted as following customer segments:

1. Cluster 1: Clients having medium annual income and lower annual spending.
2. Cluster 2: Clients having high annual income with medium to high annual spending.
3. Cluster 3: Clients having low annual income.
4. Cluster 4: Clients having medium annual income but high annual spending.

As you can see the cluster 4 is straightaway a potential customer segment. At the same time the cluster 2 and 3 could be segmented further to reach at a particular targeted client group. Now let's see how the clusters are created when we take k=6.

#Fitting kmeans to the dataset - k=6

km4=KMeans(n_clusters=6,init='k-means++', max_iter=300, n_init=10, random_state=0)

y_means = km4.fit_predict(X)

#Visualizing the clusters

plt.scatter(X[y_means==0,0],X[y_means==0,1],s=50, c='purple',label='Cluster1')

plt.scatter(X[y_means==1,0],X[y_means==1,1],s=50, c='blue',label='Cluster2')

plt.scatter(X[y_means==2,0],X[y_means==2,1],s=50, c='green',label='Cluster3')

plt.scatter(X[y_means==3,0],X[y_means==3,1],s=50, c='cyan',label='Cluster4')

plt.scatter(X[y_means==4,0],X[y_means==4,1],s=50, c='magenta',label='Cluster5')

plt.scatter(X[y_means==5,0],X[y_means==5,1],s=50, c='orange',label='Cluster6')

plt.scatter(km.cluster_centers_[:,0], km.cluster_centers_[:,1],s=200,marker='s', c='red', alpha=0.7, label='Centroids')

plt.title('Customer segments')

plt.xlabel('Annual income of customer')

plt.ylabel('Annual spend from customer on site')

plt.legend()

plt.show()

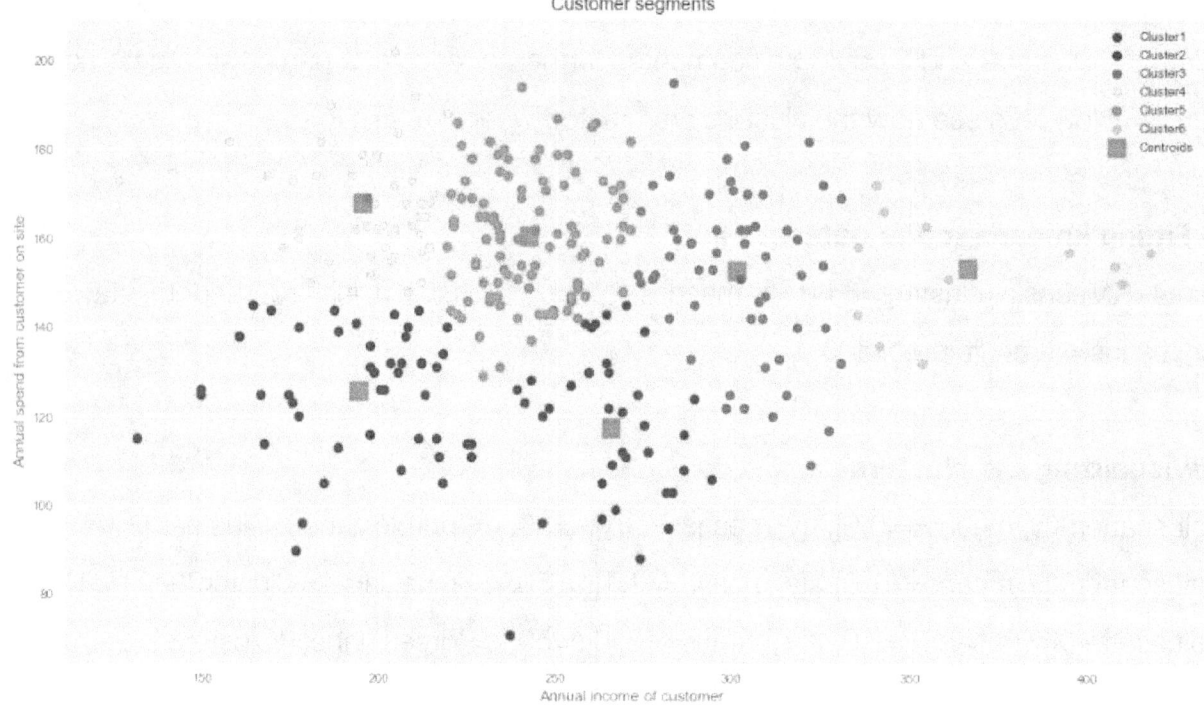

Cluster Plot: k=6

By setting the number of clusters to 6 it paved the way for a more meaningful client segmentation.

1. Cluster 1: Medium income and low annual spending.
2. Cluster 2: Low income and low annual spending.
3. Cluster 3: High income and high annual spending.
4. Cluster 4: Low income and high annual spending.
5. Cluster 5: Medium income and low annual spending.
6. Cluster 6: Very high income and high annual spending.

It is evident from the data above that 6 clusters provide a more useful segmentation of clients.

Marketing Strategies for Different Customer Segments

Based on these 6 cluster some marketing strategies could be formulated which were relevant to every cluster.

A common strategy would be to focus on some promotional efforts for high value clients of cluster 6 and cluster 3.

Cluster 4 is unique. In this customer segment despite their low annual income the clients tend to spend more on the website thereby showing their loyalty. There was a possibility of some discounted pricing based campaigns for the group in order to retain them.

A further analysis was needed for cluster2 where both the annual income and spending was low. The reason for the low spending needed to be determined and price sensitive strategies had to be introduced to raise spending from the segment.

The clients from clusters 1 and 5 are not spending enough on the website despite earning a solid annual income. Further analysis was needed about these segments to find out the satisfaction and dissatisfaction levels of the clients. A possibility of less visibility of the products or the site to them had to be considered. Strategies had to be evolved accordingly.

So, there you are. We saw how we could arrive at meaningful insights and recommendations by using the clustering algorithms to create the client segments. Here for the sake of simplicity in understanding the data set made use of just 2 variables viz income and spending. In the actual business scenario there are many variables that could generate even more realistic and more business specific insights for the managers.